The Overcoming Life Through Prayer

Nita Johnson
Copyright ©1988 by Nita Johnson
Second publication under new title
"The Overcoming Life Through Prayer" 1998
Printed in the United States of America
ISBN: 0-9656528-3-1

Edited by: *Ricci Wilson*
Cover design and
Desktop Publishing by:
            Gary Grubbs
            Freestyle Graphics
            1334 S. 119th St. • *Suite B*
            Omaha, NE 68144

DEDICATION

To my daughter Ricci, who although is now a wife and mother of four is still my precious jewel and has given of herself for the completion of this book. Who also is the joy and love of my heart! To my mother. And to all those who want to live as overcomers in Christ.

The author's cassette tape series on future events concerning the Body of Christ, America, Israel, and the world are available from:

The World For Jesus Ministries, Inc.
Nita Johnson
World For Jesus Ministries
MSC #402
497 N. Clovis Ave. #202
Clovis, CA 93611-0373

CONTENTS

FORWARD

by Dick Eastman

Less than twenty-four hours after returning from the Islamic stronghold of Malaysia where it is still a serious crime to witness to a Moslem, I picked up the manuscript to *"The Overcoming Life Through Prayer"*. Within minutes I knew the timing was not merely coincidental.

So many books on prayer are all alike, and I was reluctant to read still another. Much to my surprise, however, I quickly discovered *"The Overcoming Life Through Prayer"* is strikingly unique. Chapters like "Humility, A Divine Treasure Chest" and "The Gift of Obedience" touched my heart as if I were hearing a personal word from the Lord. It was a word that contained keys to help keep me from falling into the tragic trap of that deadly sin of spiritual pride that is the root of so much sin.

The very day I began reading this timely challenge coincided with the final day of a very special forty day fast, a fast during which God promised to open my eyes to the invisible realm as never before. Surely my reading *"The Overcoming Life Through Prayer"* on the day that fast concluded is a significant part of that answer.

Nita Johnson's revelation insights contain fresh manna from the ovens of heaven. Repeatedly, I found myself underlining scriptural insights that I had never noticed or concepts that I had just barely begun to grasp.

Beloved, I commend to you this challenge on how to prepare for victorious warfare. But please don't read it too hastily. Tarry with the Lord over every chapter and ask Him to give you even further revelations. And may I suggest you do as I do—underline thoughts for later meditation, and write little notes to yourself in the margins of each page as God speaks to you.

You will quickly discover this is not just a book. It is a message from the Lord—especially for you. Don't miss a word of that message. It will help you change your world.

Dick Eastman
Change The World Ministries
P. 0. Box 5838
Mission Hills, CA 91345

Editor's Note:
Dick Eastman is the developer of the *Change the World School of Prayer* seminars and other training resources on prayer that have now been used by over 100 different denominations, in more than 120 nations, touching well over 1,000,000 believers.

INTRODUCTION

Perhaps you've always struggled with prayer. Or, like so many, perhaps prayer has always been the thing you do during the last five minutes of your day "whether you need it or not." One person said: "Prayer is like medicine: good for what ails you——but who likes medicine?"

That statement may typify the view held by about 90 percent of all Christians. If prayer is anything but exciting to you, this book may change your mind. And, if you are willing, you may be embarking on a wonderful adventure.

Praying people are much needed in the Kingdom of God. This book will guide you in working through the various hindrances in prayer. I trust it will give you the strength to persevere until you see victory. I'll be sharing many of my prayer experiences, my struggles, and the mistakes I have made as I learned the valuable lessons of walking in love.

This is a book of technique. When an individual abides by the principles of prayer, it is impossible for him or her to fail because God's promises are true and unchanging.

In past years, there has been little balance of truth. The pendulum, so to speak, has swung wildly between indifference to the moving of the Holy Spirit—or outright rejection and untamed wildfire as people ran after signs and wonders, not wanting the discipline of the complete Word of God.

The Lord spoke to me about this. He said: "There is a new group of prophets being released in the Church. They will proclaim what will seem to be a new thing, however, it will be a revival of the old and will prepare the way for the new revelations of the eleventh hour." This will prepare us for an unprecedented display of the living Christ, one that will impact the world as none other.

What will be proclaimed? Truths—given to the apostles by the Holy Spirit that we have yet to unveil. And who are these prophets? They are men and women who have spent years in intimate fellowship with God, drinking from the Holy Spirit. When they open the Word, the nature and character of God is revealed clearly because they know Him. They are not fearful of truth, so they are not cold to the Spirit's ways. But they have such a deep reverence for God that they honor Him with true order and obedience—having the fire but containing it within the boundaries of God's order. These people love pure truth and carefully balance their teachings.

This new welling-up of balanced truth will refresh the Body of Christ. It will come from people who "know their God" through the intimate communion found in prayer. After spending time as one of God's intercessors, you may find that you too have been called as one of these prophets.

My main goal Dear Reader, in giving you this writing however, is to encourage you to enter the overcoming life, which can only be accomplished through prayer. What is the overcoming life? It is the life of one who has been made inwardly into Christ's own image. Once you have appropriated this wonderful grace you will reflect the fruits of the Spirit in lush and ripened expression in your life. Being thus perfected you will bring great glory to Jesus while never touching the glory that belongs only to Him. Because you will have been taught to walk in God's own love, you will have overcome all fear, flesh and the devil.

A life such as this is not only possible, but is God's earnest desire for all that belong to Him. We can never reach such a lofty plateau in our own strength, but with the help and grace of God, it is more than possible to achieve. If you have an intimate walk with Him now, you are a prime candidate.

The Father once asked me if I would like to know and love Him as Jesus did when He was here on this earth, sharing the communion they shared. Naturally, I would give anything to walk with my heavenly Father in this way. One who enters into the overcoming life is granted entry into this high and holy experience. Jesus further told me that anyone who wants to walk in this much-desired place may! If you are willing to pay the price to leave the world behind in exchange for the secrets of His glory.

PART I

Perseverance

The first part of this book is about *perseverance*—how to get it and maintain it, even against incredible odds.

Your heart will be encouraged to know that nothing is impossible with God, and no goal is out of reach to those who won't quit. (See Matthew 19:26.)

Scripture tells us over and over again that the key to success for anything in the Lord is perseverance. Without it we are merely spiritual sprinters in a long distance race. We won't last! With perseverance there is no limit to what you can become in God. Neither education, nor intelligence, nor any other thing that pertains to the flesh can determine the heights to which we can go in the overcoming life. Perseverance, in faith alone sets your destiny. The Lord once told me: "Put your will to the race and your faith will go before you and overcome the obstacles." God desires to bring us to this lofty place of abundance. We must have a burning desire to enter!

Chapter 1 —————————————————

Mountains Are Meant To Be Overcome

Stop and look around your world. What do you see? Is everything the way you always dreamed it would be? Is there anything you would like to change but thought was impossible?

How are your children doing? Did you ever consider that their future could be molded by your prayers? Now think about your spouse. Is your marriage fulfilling?

Before you shrug your shoulders and say that it's hopeless to dream about things being different, I want to tell you a true story. I have a friend named Shirley who is a good wife to her husband and the mother of five children. Her husband, however, had begun to take her for granted. Shirley tried desperately to change the situation, but she only met with failure. In a state of total discouragement she said to herself: "Since all else has failed, the only thing left to do is pray." So Shirley went through her Bible and pulled out five of the most appropriate scriptures she could find. Each morning and evening she would go to a place by herself and pray these scriptures. Shirley always concluded her time with the Lord by praising Him for the beautiful relationship and new excitement she and her husband would soon enjoy.

About two months after she began this practice, I visited with Shirley over lunch. When I asked about her marriage, her eyes sparkled as she eagerly shared the new romance she and her husband were experiencing. Taking my arm, she led me into the living room. As we entered, I noticed that the room was newly furnished.

"Nita," she said: "My husband had saved for months to buy a new truck. Instead, he took all the money, went down to the furniture store on Saturday, and bought me this brand new living room set. I didn't even know what he had done until it arrived at the house that afternoon."

Shaking her head, Shirley continued: "I was excited because I have wanted this set for a long time. But at the same time, I was concerned that this purchase would mean the loss of the truck he needed. When I expressed this to him, he kissed me and said: "Honey, knowing how much this means to you and how much you'll enjoy it will do more for me than a new truck would ever do."

After all the "oo's" and "ah's," Shirley and I went back to the kitchen to finish lunch. Then Shirley laid her hand upon my arm and said: "Nita, prayer really does change things."

But that was not the end of the story. Visiting her again about four months later, I learned that Shirley's husband got the very truck he wanted for $2000 less than he had expected to pay. She and I both knew it was the Lord's doing. As far as their marriage is concerned, it is getting better all the time.

A valuable lesson emerges from such experience; you can't look for someone else to do your praying for you. God wants to make miracles happen through you, regardless of your age, background, experience in prayer, or lack of it. God desires to use anyone who will make themselves available. You can begin right now just by making the commitment.

Like everything else, the overcoming life begins with the first step. Shirley could have spent the rest of her life brooding and bitter. But, she chose instead to pray and trust the Lord. In whatever current circumstances you find yourself, God wants to lift you to new victories if you will pray in faith and let Him teach you His ways while He works to answer your prayers.

A CHANGE OF DESTINY

When she was but twelve years old, my daughter Ricci's best friend suddenly turned away from following the Lord. She also quit communicating with Ricci, who was also twelve. This, of course, broke my daughter's heart.

After a few weeks, Ricci came to me and asked if I thought it would do any good for her to go on a twenty-four-hour fast and use that time to pray for her friend.

Amazed at her determination, I asked her to think hard about making such a commitment, twenty-four hours is a long time for a twelve-year-old to go without food. She came back a few minutes later and asked: "Mom, do you think God will answer my prayer if the reason I want her to come back to Jesus is so I can have her as a friend again?"

Smiling, I kissed her forehead and answered: "I think you and Jesus feel the same way, honey. I have a feeling you both want her back as a friend."

With that, she started her fast and began to pray. It was a long, grueling twenty-four hours—topped off with a super-deluxe combination pizza.

Ricci waited patiently for her friend to call. As hours rolled into days and then weeks, Ricci kept praying and believing. Nearly three weeks went by.

Finally, the long-awaited call came. I could hear Ricci in the living room, crying and laughing at the same time as she and her friend talked. The conversation lasted for hours, and Ricci's joy was bubbling over.

Later that night, she said to me: "Mom, me and Jesus got our friend back. We sure are glad! Aren't you?"

My "mother's heart" rejoiced with my daughter. God used the prayer of a child to change the destiny of another child. Don't ever think God won't use you or doesn't need you. The Lord said:

Whatsoever ye shall ask the Father
in my name, he will give it you.

Hitherto [up to now] have ye asked
nothing in my name: ask, and ye
shall receive, that your joy may be
full—John 16:23,24.

Jesus didn't say you had to be well-versed in the Scriptures. Neither did He say that you have to reach a certain pinnacle of spirituality before God will use you to change the world around you. The only criteria Jesus gave was to ask in His name. I am further reminded that Jesus commented on our need to be as little children in respect to our relationship with Him. As time passes, you my Dear Reader will come to see that as the Lord is busy answering those well directed prayers. He is also in the process of fulfilling His own heart's desire concerning us. His desire is threefold. First, He is helping us to shift our dependence from ourself to Himself. Second, year by year we are becoming more like a little child in innocence before Him if we are maintaining a prayer life, and not living in rebellion to Him. Third, we are steadily becoming more dangerous to the enemy.

A HOPELESS SITUATION?

Some people don't pray because they look at a situation and decide it's hopeless. We decide that a certain person is "too set in his ways" or that a given situation is fixed.

Jesus spoke to this issue when He said: *"With men it is impossible, but not with God: for with God all things are possible"* (Mark 10:27, italics added).

Everything that happens in this world—the natural realm—first happens in the spiritual realm. Your job is to pull those good things that God has prepared for you from the spiritual realm to the natural realm, where you can enjoy their benefits. How is this done? By prayer. Prayer makes the impossible possible every day.

The Lord told Elijah to go to a widow's house in Sidon, for He had commanded her to feed the prophet. Yet in verse twelve the widow said she was preparing her last meal of food, after which she expected to die. (See 1 Kings 17:9.)

It took Elijah's obedience to bring the spoken promise of provision into the physical. Furthermore, although the widow was unaware of God talking to her, He had put the faith in her heart to obey the prophet. This brought the Lord's provision from the spiritual realm into the natural realm in the form of a miracle for both of them. God caused her jar of oil and container of meal to remain full until the famine was over.

The Bible abounds with such examples. Christ is the *"Lamb slain from the foundation of the world" (Revelation 13:8)*. Yet we know that in the natural this didn't take place until nearly two thousand years ago. The writer to the Hebrews says:

> *"THOU HAST PUT ALL THINGS IN SUBJECTION UNDER HIS FEET." For in subjecting all things to him, He left nothing that is not subject to him. But now we do not yet see all things subjected to him—Hebrews 2:8 NASB.*

It has been proclaimed that the work is done, but we do not yet see the completed picture in the natural realm. The Lord gave Abraham the land we call Israel several thousand years ago. Yet he, like many others, died without seeing the tangible fulfillment of the promise. (See Hebrews 11:13.)

The Bible tells us that God *"calls things that are not as though they were" (Romans 4:17 NIV)*. Then we learn that we receive them by *faith* and *obedience*. (See Hebrews 4:6; 11:1.) James 4:2 says: *"Ye have not because ye ask not,"* yet the Bible says the Father has already made a way where there seems to be no way.

The Bible isn't giving conflicting reports. It's simply saying that God has made provisions for us. Things happen in the spiritual realm first because God is Spirit. Then we bring those provisions into the natural realm through prayer and supplication where we can enjoy them.

If you look around and don't like what you see, make the commitment to see your life change through prayer.

A friend of mine, Melinda, told me about a time she met with what seemed to be an impossible situation.

When Melinda and her mother were visiting some relatives, Melinda discovered that her cousin Virginia, apparently had an immovable problem. Her husband Sam, had been an alcoholic for years and had developed a neurotic phobia about crowds. Although his wife asked him to go to church with her week after week, he always refused. His heart was hardened toward God.

When the visit was over, Virginia stepped up to Melinda's car to say goodbye. Suddenly, she said: "Will you pray that my husband will go to church tonight?" After praying for over three years, Virginia was well aware of all the obstacles that needed to be overcome. Regardless, it was clear to Melinda that her cousin was not about to give up.

Virginia had already gone back in the house when Melinda and her mother began to pray. Immediately, Melinda saw a wonderful vision of Sam and other family members going up to the altar of the church to give their lives to Christ. Then she saw all these family members congregating at Sam and Virginia's home that evening after church.

In the meantime, Virginia had decided to ask Sam once more about going to church. Much to her surprise, he responded with a hearty yes! Virginia went running out of the house to share the good news. When she reached the car, Melinda told her all that the Lord had shown her.

That night, Virginia was amazed as she watched the vision unfold before her eyes. Her husband and many other family members were saved, and Sam was delivered from alcoholism and his phobia of large crowds. They concluded the evening by congregating at Sam and Virginia's home. It was a triumphant climax to three long years of prayer.

GOD'S MOUNTAIN MOVERS

God is in the mountain moving business. He did it Himself when He created earth, and He's been doing it ever since. Now, however, God works through His vessels—people like you and me. Jesus said:

> Whosoever shall say unto this mountain, Be thou removed, and be thou cast into the sea; and shall not doubt in his heart, but shall believe that those things which he saith shall come to pass; he shall have whatsoever he saith—Mark 11:23.

Jesus is still looking for mountain movers. He is the God of the impossible, and there is no obstacle that He cannot overcome. But the Lord needs people who will believe that nothing is impossible for Him—nothing.

Jackie, a former business acquaintance, learned of a desperate situation. A mother and child had been in an automobile accident near Jackie's home in central California. The mother had escaped with minor injuries, but the baby wasn't expected to live through the night. Jackie's heart was gripped for this tiny baby, and she decided to believe God for the impossible. She phoned me and asked if I would go to the hospital with her to pray for the baby, to which I agreed.

Immediately we drove to the hospital, upon entering, Jackie and I asked the receptionist at the desk if we would be allowed to see the baby. As we expected, the woman denied us entry. Standing in the hospital corridor, we prayed silently that God would make a way. In a moment, the lady turned around and without any explanation, she said: "What are you waiting for, get going!" and directed us toward the baby's room.

We had to go through four nurse's stations. We were met with the same resistance at every one. Each time we would pray for a moment, and the nurse would turn around and tell us the directions to the baby's room.

Once in the room, tears fell from our eyes as we saw the tiny infant struggling for life. Carefully, we laid hands on the baby and prayed. Just then a nurse walked in, questioned Jackie about how we gained entrance to the room, and ordered us to leave.

Soon thereafter, Jackie called a friend who knew the child's family to see how the baby was doing. "Much to their amazement," the friend blurted: "the baby is home and doing fine!"

God has many mountain movers; Jackie is only one of them. Mountain movers must have an ingrained belief that God wants to answer their prayers. From this belief comes the needed strength to persevere.

Consider this; God knows the beginning from the end. Knowing all things, if He has allowed that mountain in our life, then it is there for our good. He will either teach us how to go around it, how to climb it, or how to cast it into the sea. Whatever the case may be, the mountain is meant to be a pinnacle of encouragement to us on our path to be an overcomer.

HITTING THE BULL'S EYE

The apostle Paul wrote to the Christians in Ephesus:

> *We wrestle not against flesh and blood, but against principalities, against powers, against the rulers of the darkness of this world, against spiritual wickedness in high places—Ephesians 6:12 .*

Martin Luther responded to this scripture with an observation of the Church as a whole, saying the real problem is that indeed: "We wrestle not." He was saying that people pray with a "take-it-or-leave-it" attitude. They pray as though they were throwing darts at a dart board. Maybe one will stick; better yet, *maybe* one will hit a bull's-eye! But, if not, at least they tried.

How shall we pray?

> *But let him ask in faith **nothing***
> ***wavering**. For he that wavereth is*
> *like a wave of the sea driven with*
> *the wind and tossed. For let not*
> *that man think that he shall receive*
> *any thing of the Lord — James*
> *1:6,7 (emphasis authors).*

Those who would move mountains cannot pray with a hit-or-miss attitude. Neither can they expect someone else to be the answer to their problem. They are the people who *refuse failure*. Years ago I heard a story I will never forget. Whenever I think of quitting, I recall this incident.

A businessman wanted to get rich by discovering oil. He owned a piece of property that had been tested, and the chances of finding oil were excellent. He left his business, bought an oil drill, and went to work. Months passed as the search for oil continued. After spending all his money, he decided to sell his home so he could invest that money in the exploration as well. Still no oil was discovered.

At last, greatly discouraged, this man decided he'd given all he was going to give to this dream. He sold the oil drill and his claim to the property to a dealer for practically nothing. Then he packed up and moved away.

The man who bought the claim and digger decided to take advantage of his new purchase. Setting up the drill exactly where the previous owner had been digging, he had drilled only a few feet when he struck oil. He died a very wealthy man, while the other man never achieved much success.

When we pray, we must not waver. *God rewards diligence.* It is the persistent prayer, like the repeated "chug, chug" of the locomotive, that gets the job done. Nothing less will do. In the arena of prayer, time is often our best friend.

Allow God to strengthen your weary heart. Relax, and let His peace rule your faith. Sit down at the bottom of that mountain, and don't stop praying until it's in the sea.

HIGHER VISTAS

If you are a person of prayer, you realize as your walk with God continues to grow that He wants to do more than just answer your prayers. Responding to your prayers is a means to a much higher end. Jesus wants to develop a relationship with His own that will result in leading each one into the overcoming life. As He helps you to build and ever-increasing dependence upon Himself, He is able to increase you in Himself. As wars are fought and victories are won, you will learn to walk with Him and yearn to abide in Him. As your yearning grows He will teach you how to overcome every obstacle that stands between you and the most cherished desire of abiding in Christ alone. Along the way Jesus will teach you of eternal values helping you to overcome the things that cannot profit which have held you ensnared perhaps for years. He does this by opening your once blinded eyes to behold the things of the Kingdom. You are then able to see their true beauty, giving enlightenment to your heart and lifting you to newer levels of faith and higher vistas of the overcoming life.

He will teach you in the way of faith, that you can overcome not only those exterior mountains, but the interior ones as well. He will shed His love abroad in your heart to strengthen you in the determination to win the greatest prize of all—that of winning Christ! As the desire of winning this most precious of all prizes consumes you, it will be just a matter of time before God will complete His lofty work in your soul and grant the zealously sought after reward—union with Christ and entrance into the overcoming life. To think it all began with prayer!

Chapter 2 ——————————————

The Victor's Wreath

Do you like to win? Do you pray to win?

I remember my parents saying: "It's not whether you win or lose that counts but how you play the game." But whenever I would lose a marble game with my brother or earn the most points for *lost* baskets in a game at school, I would walk away thinking: 'How can they believe that it doesn't matter whether you win or lose?' After all, I had just lost, which meant *someone else won.* The winner was happy, but I felt defeated.

Over the years, I have learned that there is an element of valuable truth in what my parents said. On the other hand, great strength comes from a desire to win.

Bruce Jenner made a decision to win five gold medals after a scourging, agonizing defeat at the Olympics. For the next four years, seven days a week, and many long hours a day, he strove to perfect his performance so he could win. And he did! What drove Bruce Jenner? The need to win his heart's desire. In his case, the desire to win proved productive and rewarding.

The desire to win, if purged and purified of selfish ambition, can be a powerful tool when directed by the Holy Spirit. The apostle Paul expressed his greatest desire throughout his writings. He said: *"I have suffered the loss of all things, and do count them but dung, that I may **win Christ"** (Philippians 3:8, italics added).*

Paul also sought to *win* the lost—at the risk of his own life; and he sought to win his brothers, the Jews, at the cost of his own soul as he wrote: *"For I could wish that myself were accursed from Christ for my brethren, my kinsmen according to the flesh"* (Romans 9:3).

Of course, God wouldn't allow that; neither could He. Christ's blood alone could win the prize of the Jewish people whom Paul loved so dearly. Yet we see that Paul would have willingly given all that he had in material wealth and all that he was in body, mind, and soul to *win* every lost man, woman, and child to Christ.

The God-given desire to win is inherent in man's nature. Learning to channel that desire in the right direction is the key to victory. Children of God who have this rightly-directed *winner's instinct* are always thinking about pleasing their Master and heaping up glory for Him, even at the total expense of their lives. Compared with the aching hunger to hear Jesus say: *"Well done, thou good and faithful servant"* (Matthew 25:21), every other desire of their heart is tiny. That divine approval is the goal for which they constantly strive, yearn, live, and die.

The Christian who has no such burning desire is not winning because he is not straining toward a goal of receiving "praise from God." His mind has drifted from the goal; quite likely, he's not even running the race.

What a tragic moment it was for Greg Foster when he took his eyes off the goal in the 1984 Olympic hurdle race. History has forever etched in its memory how he lost the gold medal to Roger Kingdom by one-hundredth of a second—the time it took him to turn from the goal and glance to his right to see where his competition was. That simple act cost Greg the gold medal.

The apostle Paul said: *"Henceforth there is laid up for me a crown of righteousness"* (2 Timothy 4:8). In one translation this crown is called a *victor's wreath*. Paul was wise enough to keep his eyes on the goal. Will you be? The Scriptures say that God holds out to us a diadem or *crown of beauty*. The victor's wreath is a crown of beauty. Once you have completed the race victoriously, it will be the joy of Christ to place that crown upon your head.

TRAINING TO WIN

Every race is a battle. The fact that there is a crown of victory implies that there is a battle; without it there can be no victory. Someone rightly said, "Big battle, big victory." So be optimistic if your battle is a big one! There are certain strategies we can implement that will give us the decisive edge in our battle. If you were enrolled in the military, you wouldn't be allowed to head out into the front lines of battle without the proper training and equipment. This stategy is determined to, as much as possible insure success.

This is true in the world around us, and we can rest assured that it is true in the work of the Lord. God didn't call David to deliver Israel from Goliath until He taught him how to deliver his sheep from lions and bears. (See 1 Samuel 17:36.)

We can also be comforted in the fact that God is wise in His training. He never tests us above what we can bear. As Moses was leading Israel out of Egypt, the Lord did something highly unusual:

> God led them not through the way of the land of the Philistines, although that was near; for God said, Lest peradventure the people repent when they see war, and they return to Egypt—Exodus 13:17.

That meant there was only one other way to go—*through* the Red Sea! God, in His infinite mercy, chose not to take these poor slaves through a big battle. He knew that just looking at those mangy, arrogant, self-assured giants would have been enough to cause heart failure in His newly-recruited army.

The Israelites were not yet prepared for battle or equipped for victory. These former slaves, saddled with a big cloak of low self-esteem, would have been easy prey for the enemy. Rather than subject them to a battle for which they weren't ready, the Lord took them through the Red Sea. There He instead gave them a magnificent miracle. In short, God prepares His children every step of the way for each new victory they will win.

On the other hand, the Bible does tell us of several battles that God's people went into presumptuously. Each time they were beaten severely. (See Numbers 14.) When God leads you into battle, He will first prepare you for victory, and you will win every time. This preparation reaches its optimum only through a life of prayer, time spent in the Word daily and maintaining a posture of submission to the Lord through all things.

God also knows when the enemy will attack you and just how much time you have to prepare. Those who diligently cooperate in training and follow His leading will see many battles, but they will consider that a battle is never over until they have gained victory. As the Bible says: *"The Lord gave David victory wherever he went"* (*2 Samuel 8:6 NIV*).

In our battle to win the victor's wreath, we must be motivated by the desire to bring glory to the One who loves us. What a joy it will be to cast our crown at the feet of Jesus, knowing deep in our hearts that we would not have crossed the finish line except for Him. Until that day, however, the race is on, and the battle must be won!

You may say: "I'm not going into battle. I've accepted Jesus as my Savior, and I don't feel led to go to battle for anyone." When you came into the Kingdom of God, you stepped out of the devil's kingdom. At that moment you were targeted for a new kind of battle by the enemy—whether you liked it or not.

Knowing it is God's battle and that He has already gained the victory gives you a solid base from which to start. It is a foundation to build on—but *you* have to build on it. His victory is where we begin, not where we end.

Napoleon had an army that for many years was undefeated. One reason for this was that individually and collectively the soldiers were willing to give their lives to glorify their king. How much more should the heart of every child of the living God desire to bring honor and glory to our King on this battlefield called earth? In addition, how much more noble are the battles of righteousness. Our highest goal, the crowning victory of all battles is to know Christ, to be made into His image and to live ever-conquering the evil one who once conquered us.

MIRACLE LOVE

No price is too great to pay to win—if the prize is valuable enough. For Christ, the prize was you. So earnestly did the Lord desire you that He left the glory He had with the Father and took on the form of man. That may not mean much to us. We may think that, because He was God, it was easy for Him. But it was not easy; it took a miracle love—*agape love*—to do that.

Think about it for a moment. What would go through your mind if someone were to come to you right now and say: "My son is being held hostage. They say the ransom they want is your three year-old son." Can you feel the agony that would grip your soul? Your thoughts would begin to race: Why should I give up my son for a total stranger? Yet that's what God did.

The Bible says, *"For when we were yet without strength, in due time Christ died for the ungodly" (Romans 5:6).* The word *strength* in Greek means "without covenant." We were strangers to God, yet He sent Jesus to die for us. Why? Because His heart longed for you and me. No price was too great to have us for Himself. You didn't have to give up your child. But, God gave His Son for you and me.

What kind of amazing love did it take to cause Christ to pay the price He so willingly paid? Many Bible teachers concentrate on the physical sufferings of Jesus on the cross—He suffered terrible beatings; large thorns were gouged into His head; His back was mutilated and His bones disjointed; nails were driven through His hands and feet; and a spear was thrust through His side. For some, the reason for this emphasis on the physical is that they may be unaware of Christ's agonizing spiritual suffering.

How do you explain to human beings, who have experienced sin for as long as they can remember, what it was like for Jesus to take the sin of the world upon His pure, undefiled soul? It was one thing for Him to leave the glory He had with the Father and clothe Himself in a human tabernacle. But even that did not compare with what took place on the cross.

While meditating on this several years ago, I found myself overwhelmed by a vision of Christ on the cross and the horror that Jesus experienced taking our sins upon Himself. The physical pain alone was beyond my comprehension. How much more intense was His misery when our sin was laid upon His soul? Communion with the Father was broken, and He suffered the most unbearable emotional tearing. Jesus cried out as His heart broke and He died. Isaiah spoke truth when He called Him a man of sorrow— sorrow that you and I will never have to share.

Likewise, have you ever stopped to consider the price the Holy Spirit had to pay for our redemption? The nature of the Holy Spirit is that of a comforter, healer, and helper. His ministry is to give strength. As I look at the Holy Spirit's attributes, I am reminded of the heart of a mother.

Yet at the time when Jesus needed Him the most, God had to turn His back. He had to resist His entire nature, set it aside, and refuse to yield to the deepest agony. He could not reach out to strengthen, uplift, or heal Christ on the cross. What an anguished moment for the Godhead.

Yet beyond that moment of sorrow was the prize! The Church, in all her splendor, was now set free. Soon, like a bride, she would be dancing in His arms, arrayed with the glory that only Christ could give her. May we never forget that it took the cross and a miracle love to do it.

PASSION TO WIN

Christ had a passion to win the prize—the desire of His heart— which was redemption for you and me. Throughout eternity we will revel in the magnificent glory of His amazing love.

Implanted within us by the Holy Spirit, this same Christ-like desire to win brings us to the fullness of His strength and victory. That is the heart of the intercessor—not the winning desire of human ego but the infinitely stronger desire of divine love that will go to hell and back to win victory for the beloved.

The Holy Spirit has sounded the battle cry in the Church. He is pleading for intercessors who will make up their minds that they are going to be victorious over all the works of the enemy. God is looking for people who will pick up their swords and not stop fighting until they see the enemy defeated in the lives of those for whom they are praying.

Right now you may not have the passion of divine love to win victory for others at the total expenditure of yourself. That is something the Holy Spirit will build into you. Your only task for the moment is to make yourself available to be consumed by the zeal of this love. Don't hold back—yield yourself as a living sacrifice for such a high purpose. Then begin the work as God leads.

The Holy Spirit is saying:

> *Say not ye, There are yet four months, and then cometh harvest? Behold, I say unto you, Lift up your eyes, and look on the fields; for they are white already to harvest—John 4:35.*

When a wheat field is golden, it is overripe, causing some of the wheat to fall out of the kernels and be needlessly lost. A white harvest field means it is not just ready but desperately late—and many millions of precious souls are about to be lost eternally for lack of laborers.

Second Corinthians 6:2 says: *"Now is the accepted time; behold, now is the day of salvation"* (italics added). Now is the time for the true grit of the Holy Spirit to be manifested in us as we begin to labor on behalf of our loved ones, our community, our nation, and the world.

Let yourself become a vessel of mercy to the Body of Christ and to the lost. Go boldly to the throne of God with your prayers and supplications. Grab hold of the King of the universe and don't let go until you have made all your petitions known. Fight until you gain the victor's wreath!

In learning to intercede for others, you will become familiar with the true heart of Jesus, not only for others, but for yourself as well. The more you learn of His heart, the more perfectly you will be changed into His image. Again, intercession creates in your heart a more fertile field for the planting of the seeds of love that cause you to be willing to sacrifice whatever is needed to set your loved one free. By it, you are able to learn divine and critical lessons on behalf of our Lord's own passion. The more you are enabled to touch His passion, the greater becomes your own passion for greater victories in His name and for His glory.

By this means Jesus leads His own through the valleys to climb the most majestic mountains of faith to live the life of the overcomer. So press on! Throughout our ascent to these high precipices of faith you will gain crowns of victory over the world, the flesh, and the devil. These crowns represent your victories over the rudiments of the lower life that you will learn to hate, and your rewards of righteousness regarding the appropriation of the life of the Spirit that you will learn to love with a holy fervor. The higher the ascent, the clearer the vision grows until you able to see and understand the high nobility of the life of the Spirit creating an undying zeal to fully make it yours.

You will ascend precipices such as joy, peace, and gentleness, precipices of goodness, faithfulness, and praise. Upward the heart will aspire until it is no longer you who lives but Christ that will live in you. The world will be manifestly under your feet. Jesus will have graced you with His abiding glory, the seal of one made into His image. You will have learned to make victories in prayer—victories in Christ until at long last, He has won the whole of you. You went forth conquering and to conquer, but in the end Christ conquered you!

Chapter 3 ────────────────

Satisfying The Heart Of Jesus

Have you ever wondered how the Lord sees prayer? When the answers seem long in coming, do you wonder if God even notices your prayer?

A friend of mine, Jeff, was going through difficulties with his business a few years ago. He had been seeking the Lord in prayer for some time about these problems. When the answer wasn't forthcoming, Jeff began to ask the Lord how He saw prayer, hoping that God would give him a word of encouragement to hold on to.

That night, Jeff had an unusual dream. He saw himself on his knees praying for his family, business, friends, pastor, and church. Everything with which he was involved or concerned about was going up to the Father in prayer.

Suddenly the scene changed, and Jeff saw God the Father sitting on His throne—beside Him was Jesus. In front of them was a long line of gifts of every size and shape. Written on each gift was the word *Prayer*. One by one, the Father would draw each present to Himself and then place it on the Son's lap. Jesus would then open the present and lift out the gift. Then He would give the empty box back to the Father, who would place something new inside, wrap it back up, and send it down to earth. *By this means each prayer was answered.*

SWEET INCENSE

The Bible offers a clear and picturesque description of how God sees your prayers:

> *And another angel came and stood at the altar, holding a golden censer; and much incense was given to him, that he might add it to the prayers of all the saints upon the golden altar which was before the throne. And the smoke of the incense, with the prayers of the saints, went up before God out of the angel's hand—Revelation 8:3,4 NASB.*

Whenever I read this beautiful passage, I am reminded of the high priest of the Old Testament. Under Mosaic Law, the Jews had an intermediary between them and God—the high priest. Once a year on the Day of Atonement he entered the holy of holies to minister to the Lord and intercede on Israel's behalf.

One of the first things the high priest did was pour "sweet incense" (which had a pleasant aroma) over a *censer* or bucket full of hot coals. He then placed the censer in front of the ark of the covenant (the dwelling place of God), and the whole area was immediately filled with a cloud of beautiful fragrance. This incense was representative of the Cross and the blood of Jesus that would be shed. Everything about the priestly ritual spoke of a more perfect thing to come—the Christ.

In this typology, we see the "golden bowls full of incense" representing Jesus shed blood to be added to the prayers of the saints. In Revelations 5:8 the incense depicts the prayers of the saints. Together, the prayers of the saints and the blood of Jesus are a "sweet smelling savor" to God. Search the Scriptures to see how He responded to each sacrifice that pleased Him. Then put yourself in that person's place. Each time you pray a prayer pleasing to the Lord, He responds with joy.

From this text in Revelation we see that angels are busy guiding your prayers to Jesus. At the appropriate time, they respond to the Father and begin seeing that your prayers are answered. The richest, most powerful man on earth would naturally be able to buy or command "services" from other people for his wishes. But that service is meager compared to the kind of service and love you'll receive when you go alone to your closet to pray. As you stand before God's throne, all of heaven listens to your prayer and goes to work to perform God's well-chosen answer. So never say "nobody cares!" Remember, even in the waiting room of faith, God is teaching you Dear Reader, how to be an overcomer. He is equipping you to be stalwart to the detriment of your enemy!

SATISFYING THE HEART OF JESUS

Unfortunately, we don't always see prayer in such a happy light. When I first started my prayer life, I felt frustrated. I wanted God desperately, yet I lived with an underlying feeling that my communion wasn't equally important to Him. Have you ever felt that way? Consequently, prayer was often a struggle. I used to say: "God, if You only knew how much I want You, You wouldn't make it so difficult for me to have the kind of fellowship I so desire to have with You."

One evening I sat down to spend some time with my family. While I sat engrossed in watching my family interplay with one another, the Lord spoke to my heart: "If only you could know that I want you so much more than you could *ever* want Me!"

Silent tears began trickling down my face. How could I ever have doubted His great love? I knew I would never struggle in prayer again. I said quietly, "I love You, Lord."

God is always ready to love you and fellowship with you. He waits with great expectancy until the next time He can help you. The Lord loves it when the Holy Spirit can lead you closer to Himself.

One morning I was preparing to spend some time with the Lord. Just as I sat down in front of the large window overlooking a lake, (my favorite place to pray), He sang to me in my spirit, "Precious and few are the moments we two can share." It touched my heart deeply. I replied: "Lord, I'm glad that in the world to come it won't be moments but rather eternity." I then experienced a beautiful time of fellowship with Jesus.

I spend quality time with God every day. Yet to Him they are like fleeting moments. How many husbands feel that way about their wives? (We are the Bride of Christ!) But that is Jesus' nature—He is tender, sensitive, and caring. Jesus desires to reveal these special qualities of His to anyone who will take time to develop an intimate relationship with Him.

How important are the times of communion you share with Jesus? To Him, they are precious. He said: *"Learn from me"* (*Matthew 11:29 NIV*). What an exciting invitation! What would you do if Jesus was standing in front of you right now? If He reached out His nail-scarred hand and tenderly said: "Come, learn from Me," wouldn't you go anywhere He wanted to lead?

That is exactly what Jesus Christ does through His Word. He has asked you to leave the world behind. It is only through prayer and those valuable moments in the Word that you can learn to walk with the Master.

Have you ever wondered why Jesus beckons us to learn from Him? If you think it was so you would go out and win the world for Him, you are wrong. He has an insatiable thirst for fellowship and complete ownership of each of us.

I could spend three hours a day in prayer. That would bring Jesus great joy; however, it wouldn't satisfy His thirst for *you*. On the other hand, you could spend three hours a day in prayer. Although it would always bring Him great pleasure, it would not satisfy His hunger for me. The Lord needs time with each and every one of His children.

On the cross, extended between the earth and heaven, Jesus Christ uttered a cry. He was only moments from death, yet from

the depths of His soul came the words: *"I thirst"* *(John 19:28)*.
Thinking he had something to satisfy the longing of a desperate soul, one of the men standing below Him dipped a sponge in vinegar and offered it to Jesus. What he didn't know was that Christ was uttering the cry of mankind to a God who seemed far away.

Christ the Man was crying: "I thirst for You, God." Those words were uttered so all who would follow could be satisfied. And Christ, our God, was crying out the passion that drove Him to the cross, saying: "I thirst for you, My children."

How sweet those words. How sweet the knowledge that our God "thirsts" for us. Will His thirst for you be satisfied?

THE SECRET TO VICTORY

Psalm 16:11 boldly declares: *"In thy presence is fullness of joy."* One of the richest rewards of an ongoing prayer life is the joy that begins to dominate your life.

Before I accepted the Lord as my Savior, I battled with depression. I was not constantly depressed, but the battle was at times constant. Sometimes I would win, and sometimes I would lose. The Lord did not suddenly and miraculously heal me of this problem even after my salvation. I did, however, find a cure.

When I gave my life to Christ, I was awakened to an insatiable hunger for the Word and for prayer. Knowing nothing about either one, I just plunged right in. Although prayer was a struggle at first, the struggle soon gave way to a sense of delight and well-being. It took about six months before I realized that I wasn't struggling so much with depression any more. Instead, a new underlying joy was becoming prevalent.

I must also tell you that, during this period of my life, the struggles outside my prayer closet were growing in intensity. All around me, life seemed like a storm-driven sea. Yet I was getting stronger. Peace and joy became the ship of refuge that held me secure. The storm lasted many years, going from one degree of intensity to another. People around me would ask, "How is it that you are so strong? Most people don't even know what you're going through because of the incredible way you're handling everything!"

Credit must be given where credit is due. Had these problems all happened before my salvation, I never would have made it. I told my friends the same thing I'm going to tell you: I made it through victoriously only because of the time I spent in the Word and prayer.

Victory comes from living in God's presence. We begin to develop joy as we enter His presence on a consistent basis, experience His love, and see His power repeatedly break through to victory. It also comes by the work of faith that is ever growing through the instrumentality of God's grace. When you get in touch with the source of joy on a consistent basis, you will be wonderfully transformed by its power.

The friend I mentioned earlier, Melinda, was hit by a terrible bout of depression some years ago. She finally got fed up with it and retired to her room, where she spent most of three days "praising the Lord." All this time she felt miserable, but she was determined to prevail. The third night she came into such joy that she thought she had been raptured. She walked in the strength of that joy for many, many months.

The Bible says: *"You have made known to Me the ways of life; You will **enrapture** Me—diffusing My soul with joy—with and in Your presence"* (Acts 2:28 Amplified, italics added).

The Lord once let me feel what is going to occur the moment we are raptured. When we are caught up to meet Jesus in the air it will be by the power of His joy. But God isn't saving the best for last. He wants us walking in the power of His joy *now*. How do we get it? By walking in the energy of a life dominated by the Word and prayer and with an attitude of praise and worship to the King of Joy.

In His presence there is fullness of joy. Joy is not only the outgrowth of a healthy prayer life but the fuel of prosperous prayer.

THE VALUE OF JOY

John Hyde was an accomplished prayer warrior. He prayed ministries into new dimensions, souls into the Kingdom of God, and revival into India. Needless to say, John Hyde's life was anything but dull. Daily he spent long hours in prayer, pleading for souls. These prayer times were usually followed by fruitful soul-winning sessions.

At one point in his life, however, John Hyde seemed to have lost his touch. He prayed and faithfully went out to reap the harvest from his morning intercession, only to return home bewildered over the lack of fruit in so many hours of painstaking effort. Tearfully, he sought the Lord for the answer to his problem.

After a few days, God's surprising response came. The Lord said: "John, you've lost your joy!" Relieved by the simplicity of the Lord's admonition, John Hyde quickly revived his joy. Then he set out to gain his heart's prize—the souls that were to be his reward.

Embodied in faith is joy! Just as a car cannot move without gas, faith is powerless when its tank is empty of joy. Inherent in joy is *expectancy.*

Can you imagine receiving a long-awaited new car and getting depressed? Try to visualize sitting in your living room waiting to hear your new car is ready to pick up—come and get it! Your heart is beating rapidly, and you feel as though you will explode with joy. You can already smell the new interior and feel your hands gripping the wheel. And, oh, what a beauty! You can almost hear the "oo's" and "ah's" of your friends and family, and you're soaring. Why? Because it's yours. Even though the car is not yet in your driveway, you know it's yours. Your heart is full of expectancy, for possession is just a matter of time.

That is how joy works in regard to prayer. Joy gives you the strength to *wait out* answers to prayer. It releases the dynamics of faith and holds you firm—anchored deeply in the promise until the storm passes and the answer is in your hand.

Joy is the strength of your faith. God finds great pleasure in a saint who joyfully expects Him to fulfill His promises. Such faithful expectation is a sign of maturity. When you refuse to let go of your joy, it becomes a wall of defense around the cherished prize. Satan can't steal it if he can't get to it.

A couple of years ago I went on a lengthy fast. About two weeks into the fast, I suddenly became weak. I was concerned that I wouldn't be able to continue. When I sought the Lord for an explanation, He led me to Nehemiah 8:10: *"The joy of the Lord is your strength."* Realizing that I had lost my joy, I decided that Satan wasn't going to defeat me—I'd finish the remaining two weeks of my fast in *joy*. My strength returned, I reached my goal, and God richly rewarded me for my labor.

When you have developed the *attitude of gratitude*, you find your relationship with God and man changes. Joy prevails, and a rich ongoing current of power is at your disposal to defeat the enemy.

When your relationship with God is based on thanksgiving instead of constant rehearsals of disappointments, it brings Him more pleasure, too.

Chuck, a friend of mine, had planned a special trip. Things didn't go as planned, and consequently, his trip had to be cancelled. He cried and carried on all night because of his disappointment, continually asking the Lord why He was never there when He was needed.

Early in the morning, Jesus appeared to Chuck and rebuked him for his attitude. After telling Chuck he would soon find out why the trip had been cancelled, the Lord turned to walk away. Then, as an afterthought, Jesus looked at Chuck again and said: "By the way, I don't ever want to spend another night like that with you again." With that, He left. Later, Chuck learned that the plane on which he had been scheduled had crashed! Jesus had spared his life.

The attitude of gratitude stirs our joy to new heights, releases us into exciting times with the Lord, and frees joy to anchor us into a solid faith that turns problems into blessings.

In all things that the Lord allows to enter our lives, He is carefully developing in us divine virtues. Like a master sculptor He is producing in us a steadfastness that gives birth to and sustains endurance. Many years ago the Lord warned me through a series of dreams and visions that I was going to travel through a long season of severe trials. I was frightened, so I pleaded with Him for some encouragement. In response to my pleas, He gave me a diamond studded wedding ring. As He placed it upon my wedding finger, I noticed that the diamonds spelled "wishing you thankfulness". That was my word of strength.

Don't fear, only rejoice as nothing can hurt us when we are in Christ. Every trial, when in the strength of prayer will only make us stronger, giving us hinds feet for the high places of the overcoming life.

PART II

Overcoming Hindrances

The second part of this book is aimed at overcoming the hindrances to a healthy, powerful prayer life.

Developing strong "prayer muscles" can be as difficult and tedious as strengthening flabby biceps that are weak from disuse. You can, however, learn certain principles that will make this process much easier and faster.

I urge you to take hold of these principles and don't let go until you have entered the "overcoming life."

Chapter 4 ————————————

You're Forgiven

A few years ago, I watched one of the most tragic scenarios I have ever seen unfold. Carrie, a friend of mine, was dying of cancer. I fasted, prayed, and cried for her soul, pleading with her to accept Jesus as her Savior and Healer. The closer death came and the more imminent its demand, the more positive she became that God could never forgive her. Although she would never tell me what horrible sin she had committed that rendered her "unforgivable," Carrie never wavered from her stand. I watched her once healthy body waste away until all that remained was a frail little skeleton.

Carrie was loved by all who knew her. I couldn't imagine how she could have been so trapped in the wretched deception that claimed her soul. In the years that followed, I often wondered if the very guilt that took her soul might have been the source of her cancer. Carrie wanted God, but guilt was an immovable mountain that stood between her and the One she needed so desperately.

Why is it that some hearts want God and want to see His power in their lives, yet they seem to live in a powerless vacuum? The answer is simple but true——their prayer life is powerless and ineffective.

Prayer, like anything else in life, must be rooted in a solid foundation. If not, it will topple with the slightest wind. What is this foundation? It's the understanding of what happened the day you were born again. You were transformed from being lost, wicked, and foolish and given new life in Christ. In Him you are redeemed, righteous, and wise. (See 1 Corinthians 1:30.) Did you know that? Then why don't you feel like a "spiritual superhero?"

Most people, before salvation, were not nice. Sure, some were sweet, kind, and sensitive——their worst sin was telling a "little white lie." For the most part, however, people come from backgrounds full of problems. Some have committed crimes against society, such as prostitution, theft, murder, or embezzlement; others have wrestled with more personal problems, such as alcoholism or drug abuse.

Whatever your background was, this chapter will address fundamental truths that will enable you to walk in greater liberty with Christ *today*. In turn this will allow you to become the overcomer you are meant to be.

Jesus said:

> *Everyone who comes to Me, and* **hears** *My words, and acts upon them, I will show you whom he is like: he is like a man building a house, who dug* **deep** *and laid a* **foundation** *upon the rock; and when a flood rose, the torrents burst against that house and* **could not shake it,** *because it had been well built—Luke 6:47,48 NASB,* **italic added.**

So the way to enjoy a "well-built house" is to *come* to Jesus, *hear* His words, and *do* His words thereby digging deep until you have found the Rock upon which to build your foundation. Then, the storm cannot destroy your house.

Where do you think Satan tries to stop God's children in this process? His first and most powerful attempt is to stop you from hearing God's Word. Let's investigate why.

The Greek word for "hear" has a more expanded meaning than it does in English. It means to *hear and understand.* How can you be obedient to the Word if you don't have a full understanding of it? The New Testament word "hear" also carries the connotation of receiving. You must hear, understand, and *receive* the word.

We can compare this spiritual principle to a kitchen sieve that can receive water but can't hold water; the water runs right through it. On the other hand, a quart jar can both receive and hold the water. This is what Jesus meant when He said to hear the Word. You are to hear, understand, and receive it by holding it in your life.

Many people in the church have memorized scores of verses, but they don't understand the God behind the Scriptures. As a result, they are without the foundation needed to assure a strong, healthy Christian life.

In the parable mentioned above, Jesus said *when* the flood arose, not *if*. Understanding where we stand with Christ is critical if we are to understand who we are in Him. Only when we are equipped with this knowledge will we be able to withstand the enemy's floods.

Our confidence in the arena of prayer, therefore, never rests in ourselves but in the One who redeemed us. The full understanding of that short statement is the foundation on which the house of prayer must be built.

SATAN'S FAVORITE WEAPON

One of the enemy's favorite weapons against a new prayer warrior is guilt. Unfortunately, Satan is all too effective in his efforts against God's new recruits if they don't have a solid foundation in the Word. By a solid foundation I mean an understanding of what Christ did at Calvary, as well as a life of obedience to the Word. You will soon grow discouraged under Satan's accusing finger without this foundation. In turn, you may leave the prayer closet forever.

I had only been a Christian for a few months when I began my life of prayer. Looking back, I'm sure I did many things wrong, but God moved in spite of my mistakes.

After seeing some wonderful victories and experiencing many new things with the Lord in just a few months, a new crisis suddenly arose—I needed to make a $240 car payment. I had never tackled anything quite like this and felt intimidated. The clincher was that I saw absolutely no way, naturally speaking, for the money to come in. It would take an all-out miracle.

I began to pray, and as time went on I got very bold and started taking authority over Satan. The more I prayed, the madder I got. I told the devil he wasn't going to steal from me ever again—that I would fight him and seek to destroy him for all the pain he had caused the people I loved. On and on I went for well over an hour. Boy, did I feel good when I was done.

The next day I woke up feeling totally dazed. A voice inside my head kept saying: "Who do you think you are? Does that car really mean that much to you? Does it mean more to you than I do? You say you love me, but you won't give the car up for me." The voice went on and on, and I was so naive that I thought it was God. So I started repenting. As I cried, I told God He could take the car.

Needless to say, I didn't try that tactic again for a while. Satan won that round, but he didn't win the war. The money for my car payment came in the next day. Three separate individuals brought over love gifts. As the last one was handed to me, I realized it equalled exactly what I needed! Had I known the difference between *guilt* and *conviction,* the devil would not have won even that round.

If you have ever experienced anything like what I experienced that day, you're going to love putting the enemy to flight using the following truths.

A PRIVATE AUDIENCE WITH THE KING

Picture this. As I mentioned earlier, under the Mosaic covenant the high priest of the nation of Israel entered the holy of holies once a year on the Day of Atonement. Everything he did on that day had a special significance. In effect he was acting out each year what Christ would later do "once for all" to atone for the sins of mankind.

Fully adorned in the magnificent priestly garment, the high priest would walk toward the holy of holies. This room was so named because it held within it the ark of the covenant, the special dwelling place of God among men. It was the most sacred room in the entire temple, thus only the high priest could enter.

As he walked toward the holy of holies, the high priest sprinkled the blood of a sacrificial animal on the floor before him. He would sprinkle, then step; sprinkle, then step—seven times. (See Leviticus 4:6.) By this act, he was saying: "God, I'm not coming to You on my own merit but by the blood required in Your Law."

Upon entering into the presence of God in the holy of holies, the high priest would begin to minister to God on behalf of Israel. His entrance, however, was not based upon his own righteousness but upon the mercy and righteousness of God. Today, we know that we are covered by the blood of Jesus Christ:

> *By a new and living way, which he hath consecrated for us, through the veil that is to say, his flesh; and having an high priest over the house of God; let us draw near with a true heart in full assurance of faith, having our hearts sprinkled from an evil conscience, and our bodies washed with pure water—Hebrews 10:20-22.*

This passage says that we come to God "by a new and living way." The Greek word for "new" is *prosphatos*, which is a combination of *pros* meaning "near to" and a derivative of *sphazo* meaning "to kill." The literal meaning of the whole word is "newly slain." Jesus, by His blood, provides a "newly slain" road into the heavenly holy of holies—the throne room of the Father. This ritual does not have to be done every time you want to pray. Jesus did it once and for all. By the sprinkling of His blood as He entered the heavenly holy of holies, Jesus opened that road for you. Because He is your high priest, there are no "detour" signs or "come back tomorrow" signs hanging on the door. Instead, you can have a private audience with the Lord of lords anytime you want it!

For many believers, however, something quite different happens. Let's say you decide to pray. You go into your bedroom, sit down, and immediately feel like you've been put in an interrogation chair. A voice accuses: "You're guilty! You don't pray enough. You don't read the Word enough. You don't know how to pray. Why did you yell at your daughter today?"

Does that sound familiar? More often than not, people don't withstand the accusations. They leave the prayer closet and quietly shut the door. Who wouldn't after that? If every time you went before the Father you felt like you were being put under a microscope, your nervous system would fray like an old rope. Before long you would seek your joy in other places.

But Christ has made a way for us to receive life through His Word. For it will always bring us life. The kind of condemnation that Satan brings is death.

PLANET GUILT

A born-again person should have a God-given sensitivity to any kind of wrongdoing. These signals from the Holy Spirit warn us if we are straying into spiritual danger. We must be sensitive to the "conviction" and turn quickly at the Lord's gentle rebuke. However, He never convicts us of anything from our past for which we have already repented. God's warning signals last only until we ask for forgiveness, and then He forgets we've ever sinned.

The word *guilt* in Hebrew means "an actively bad person, condemned, ungodly, a wicked man who does wrong" in other words, a man without Christ. In Greek we find some more interesting meanings: "ensnared, keeping a grudge, a place, state or time." Putting all this together, we learn that guilt is a *position*—the position of a person who has not appropriated God's forgiveness in Christ through repentance and faith. As a child of God, it is impossible to be condemned as long as we seek to live an obedient and repentant life before Him.

John 3:18 says: "He that believeth on him is not condemned: but he that believeth not is condemned already."

The Bible also says: *"The blood of Jesus Christ His Son cleanses (removes) us from all sin and guilt—keeps us cleansed from sin in all its forms and manifestations" (l John 1:7 Amplified).*

What is the prerequisite for the beautiful gift of constant forgiveness and cleansing? John says we must *"walk in the light" (verse 7)*. In other words, we must keep open communion with the Father and read and obey the Word. Further, we are told that if we *"confess our sins,"* then He is *"faithful and just to forgive us our sins, and to cleanse us from all unrighteousness" (verse 9)*.

You may say: "If it's not guilt I'm feeling when I do something wrong, then what is it?" As I already stated, guilt is not a feeling but a position. Condemnation is the feeling that a guilty person experiences after committing sin, and prior to repentance. But as an obedient child of God, you don't experience condemnation—at least not from God. Satan, not the Holy Spirit, is the accuser of the brethren.

Let me put it another way. When you were a sinner you lived on "Planet Guilt." Everyone who lives there thinks everyone else is happy, but they are deceived. Because there is no light on this planet, it is extremely dark and cold. People are sick and dying all the time. "Planet Guilt" is a miserable place to live.

When you were saved, the Holy Spirit lifted you off "Planet Guilt "and put you on "Planet Redeemed," where people are full of joy. This planet is warm and full of light. People feel loved and they desire to love.

The most wonderful part of "Planet Redeemed" is that its people are all forgiven. When someone makes a mistake or sins, they simply ask for forgiveness. The Holy Spirit then helps them over-come their weaknesses.

In Christ, there is no more feeling of condemnation for any-thing you have done in the past for which you have repented. The only thing you need to respond to is the gentle tugging of the Holy Spirit in conviction as He deals with sin currently in your life.

AMAZING GRACE

As I grew in the area of intercession, I began to purchase and read books on walking with God in prayer. It seemed that most of what I read zeroed in on the "broken and contrite heart" (Psalm 51:17). Subsequently, I began to start every day of prayer with seasons of repentance.

I thought that if this was pleasing to God, I'd do it! However, because I neglected to complete this time by remembering and thanking the Lord for being my righteousness I became more sin conscious than righteousness conscious. Soon an underlying sense of condemnation took over where peace had once lived. I looked at trials as punishment and as a physical demonstration of God's disapproval of me. I became critical of every little fault in an effort to get myself cleaned up so God could restore me to favor.

Past sins became immovable mountains that separated me from God's love and the approval that, by now, I desperately needed. I lost my joy, and depression became a constant battle. The more I repented, the more I seemed to *need* to repent. It was like being trapped in a spiritual merry-go-round.

I had lived a colorful past, to say the least; and now, instead of forgiveness, I felt tormented by the memories.

I couldn't understand what happened. Where did the sea of for-getfulness go? I would quote scriptures like: "There is therefore now no condemnation to them which are in Christ Jesus" (Romans 8:1). But the words seemed empty. Guilt had a stranglehold on me.

In one last ditch effort to be free, I put away my books and decided to study everything I could get my hands on in Greek and

Hebrew to see what the Word said about our position and relationship to the God of love, for whom I longed. Day and night I studied. As weeks melted into months, truths that brought liberty began to emerge. As long as I sought to live an obedient life, I wasn't guilty—I was forgiven! Day by day I was washed in His blood, with simple, pure repentance leading to thankfulness for God's righteousness through Christ. Peace and joy led to a new prayer life, and I began seeing greater victories than ever before.

About this time, I learned about a man named John Newton. He had been a slave trader. Packed like sardines, slaves were shipped from Africa to America on boats. As a result of Newton's ruthless brutality, many died without even the bare essentials for life. Newton considered them a people lower than animals, so any loss of life incurred by his barbaric treatment was hardly worth noticing.

In the late 1700s, however, God was listening to the prayers of a godly woman named Mama Newton. Looking right past the deed, grace reached out its loving arms into the depth of the need and saved John Newton's soul.

After years of torment he too, came to the revelation of the *grace* that saved him so long ago. As a result, he was inspired to write the song "Amazing Grace."

The relentless prayers of a mother who understood the boundless grace of Almighty God brought her son into the healing experience in which his sinful heart would be forever cleansed. He too, would become an intercessor who would etch in history's memory the matchless wonder of grace that was the testimony of his life.

A BREATH OF FRESH AIR

Jesus told his disciples quite explicitly:

> *If ye continue in my word, then are*
> *ye my disciples indeed; and ye shall*

> *know the truth, and the truth shall*
> *make you free...If the Son there-*
> *fore shall make you free, ye shall be*
> *free indeed—John 8:31,32,36.*

Why, then, is it so hard for people to understand the freedom they have when they stand in Christ Jesus? At this point, I think it's important to have a closer look at Satan, our accuser. We can best see a vivid picture of his nature through a small word study.

The Bible says: *"That enemy of yours, the devil roams around like a lion roaring [in fierce hunger] seeking someone to seize upon and devour"* (1 Peter 5:8 Amplified).

The word *devil* in Greek is *diaballo*, which literally means "to throw over or across." In classical Greek it was used of a slanderer, an accuser, or one who defamed another. It was not only used of those who would bring false charges but also of those who would deliberately and maliciously disseminate the truth concerning a man. The word "roaring" in Greek means a fierce hunger.

Second Corinthians 11:14 says that Satan *"masquerades as an angel of light"* (NIV), meaning a false portrayal of truth. Satan's game is "condemnation." Rather than coming from the heart, where God's loving warning originates, Satan's condemnation bombards the mind. In short:

> In the mask of truth he stands,
> a wretched evil spy,
> and points his finger of death,
> as he spews out his venomous lies,
> screaming, mocking, and
> angrily jeering, his attacks unmerciful,
> and terribly wearing.
> He lays his list of accusations upon
> your fettered brow:
> He has spoken so craftily that you
> have believed him somehow.
> Now like a fading flower, your peace
> and hope disappear.

Your joy in God's sweet presence
ends in disheartened tears.

Nita Johnson

The enemy of your soul paints a sad, hopeless picture. He is no respecter of persons and will assail anyone who will listen.

God is love, and He brings life. The Lord says: "I love you, so I want you to let My Holy Spirit remove this sin. You'll be much happier when it's gone." Like a mother removing a sliver from a teary-eyed youngster's finger, God takes away the sin that can only cause us pain. His "surgery" brings joy. It brings about hope and a feeling of being tenderly molded and cared for in the hands of a loving Father.

Satan, on the other hand, makes you feel condemned, hopeless, ashamed, and miserable. Often, he won't even tell you what you're feeling so badly about, so you feel like an all-around loser.

As I mentioned earlier, one of the devil's favorite tricks is to bring up your past—especially your life before salvation. Wanting you to remember everything bad you ever did, he will try to convince you that God can never use you because of your past.

Loading your spiritual gun with the knowledge that you are not guilty is the only way to fight that old dragon! If you sin, say, "Father, please forgive me"; "Jesus, please cleanse me"; and: "Holy Spirit, thank You for changing me." God will never be angry with you as long as you desire to do what pleases Him. Then turn from your sin and stay close to the Lord through prayer, the Word and an obedient life.

Boldly proclaim:

> *"I am the righteousness of God*
> *which is by faith in Jesus Christ."*
> *(See Romans 3:22 .)*
> *"I will therefore come boldly into*
> *the throne of grace, that I may*

obtain mercy and find grace to help
in the time of need." (See Hebrews
4:16.)

"He has loved me with an everlasting love." (See Jeremiah 31:3.)
(This means that God has always
loved you and you were in His
mind before He created the
world—before time began. His love
for you is from everlasting to everlasting!)

"I have confessed my sin, so He
is faithful and just to forgive my sin,
and to cleanse me from all unrighteousness." (See 1 John 1:9.)

Because you have turned from your sin and submitted to God
in righteousness, it won't be long before Satan will flee! What a
difference it will make in your relationship with the Lord and with
others.

Those wretched feelings of condemnation are one of the greatest cripplers of a prayer life. When they are removed, it will be like
taking a breath of fresh air. When you find yourself out from under
the huge weight Satan has been holding over your head, you will
experience a change in every area of your life.

DELIGHTING IN GOD

As you center your thoughts on the fact that God finds great
pleasure in you as His child, you will discover a new sense of freedom emanating from your life.

So push the accuser away, and shut your mind to his poison.
Open your mind to what God says about you. Satan is a deceiver,
and his one goal is to destroy you. He gets you started down the

path of destruction by a simple lie, and from there the snowball grows.

I found myself ministering to one of Satan's victims a few years ago. John had tried to live for God, but constant feelings of low self-worth kept him trapped in Satan's games. One sin led to another until John had fallen so far he had become possessed by demons. I met him in the midst of a crisis. After discovering that he had been involved in some adulterous affairs, his wife had given him an ultimatum—get help or get out!

As I listened to John's tragic story of failure as a man, husband, father, and Christian, it was obvious to me that he needed deliverance. It didn't take long because he wanted freedom. After he was free, John rededicated his life to the Lord and received the baptism of the Holy Spirit. He immediately made amends with his family and began the wonderful transformation that only Jesus Christ can bring. Where a once hardened bully lived, a gentle, nurturing man now flourishes. It took time, even after the deliverance; yet he learned to let the past go and reach for tomorrow!

You must forget those things which are behind and press on. In time you will no longer be burdened with the feeling that you can't meet God's expectations of you. Then, when you come into God's presence by the blood of the One who always pleases Him, you will know He is listening to you.

But don't misuse God's grace. The righteousness provided by Christ only works as long as you walk with a repentant heart, covered with His righteousness. If you want to please God and stay pure before Him, then you are truly under the cleansing blood. God will hear your prayer as if it were Jesus Himself praying. Always say: "Father, I come to you in the Name of Jesus," and in that express your confidence in God's righteousness provided for you.

At the same time, boldness in prayer also comes from knowing your own heart. (See 1 John 3:21.) You must know that you *need* Christ's righteousness. You also have to know that you've positioned yourself under that righteousness by truly wanting to please

Him. When you know that you love Him and that He has covered all your flaws and faults so that He sees you perfect, you will have complete boldness, confidence, and joy in prayer—and you will get answers!

In my earliest years of salvation, Jesus came to me, lifted me up in the Spirit and taught me the following. We all as Christians stand in *positional* righteousness. This is a gift of God's grace because of the blood of Jesus that was shed for us. However, the Lord also wants to give us *conditional* righteousness. In other words, He wants to bring us to the inner condition of being right-eous, thereby reflecting the glorious nature of the Son of God. As we desire purity, the Lord will bring us into this righteousness through repentance. In response, His love will continue to cleanse us until we have this inner purity as we sit at His feet, seek His face and turn from our sinful ways. By His powerful hand of grace Jesus will give us the power to overcome and live victoriously while on earth.

Do you see why the Bible says: *"Delight yourself in the Lord; and He will give you the desires of your heart" (Psalm 37:4 NASB)?* Trust His righteousness and stay in it by a sincere desire to please Him. Isn't that easy? It's as simple as falling in love with God. This knowledge takes all the anxiety out of prayer. You know God is hearing you; therefore, He will answer you, not because of who you are but because of *whose* you are.

From that unshakable platform you can soar into new heights of liberty, peace, and joy and seize the authority you have over Satan. You can pray powerful prayers that will produce mighty effects. Wield your sword until complete victory comes. With Christ, you cannot lose!

Further, in understanding this simple truth you will find your Christian growth take on new wings to soar. It's difficult to over-come when you are feeling overcome yourself. But when the truth of God's liberating grace pierces your heart, you will find new faith to grow and glow with Christ's redeeming love. As a result appro-priating the life of the Spirit will gradually become easier, the walk more constant, and His life in you a more pleasant reality.

Chapter 5 ————————————

Love, The Golden Rain

Love is the golden rain that feeds prayer. Without love no one can successfully and habitually live as an overcomer——with it no one can fail. Love is the source and energy of prayer and intercession.

You may say: "I love, but I fail." My response to that is: "If you love with the depth of Christ's love, you may stumble; but you will never fail." Our initial goal must be to discern and truly understand Christ's love.

In English, we use the word "love" to refer to many different feelings and emotions. In the same breath we may say: "I love pizza" and "I love my wife." The Greek language, however, provides for the obvious differences. And since the New Testament was written mostly in Greek, we can discover what God has to say about love.

The two types of love most commonly found in the New Testament are *phileo* and *agape*. Two types of love less commonly found but which play an important role in today's society are *stergein* and *eran*.

An understanding of these different types of love is essential to this discussion. Beginning with the latter, we find:

Eran (not found in New Testament writings), in common language, is a word used by the Greeks to speak of a sexual love. In its purest form, however, *eran* is a love of an over-mastering passion that seizes and absorbs into itself the whole mind. In Christian writings it was depicted as a God kind of love.

Stergein is a love of natural affection. Parents have it for children, and children have it for parents. Husbands and wives feel this love for one another. This quiet, abiding feeling within causes delight in the heart of its bearer by the recognition of the object loved: when you feel comforted by the sound of your husband tenderly saying: "I love you" or "you're wonderful"; or when you arrive home and your three-year-old comes running with arms outstretched, anxious to be gathered once again in the arms of love and protection. Such encounters put a new song in your heart as both giver and receiver experience the arousal of *stergein* love.

Phileo refers to gentleness and goodness toward mankind——an affection one would have for another of similar qualities or interests. It is a love based on the pleasure that the object loved gives to the possessor of that love. This is a love of need!

Agape looks upon its object as a prize and is awakened by the sense of great value in the object loved. It stirs in the heart of its bearer the desire of self-sacrifice to meet the need of the one loved. *Agape* is the love with which Christ loves us. A giving love, it is the love that "never fails":

> *Love is patient, love is kind. It does*
> *not envy, it does not boast, it is not*
> *proud. It is not rude, it is not self-*
> *seeking, it is not easily angered, it*
> *keeps no record of wrongs. Love*
> *does not delight in evil but rejoices*
> *with the truth. It always protects,*
> *always trusts, always hopes,*
> *always perseveres. Love never*
> *fails——1 Corinthians 13:4-8*
> *NIV.*

Phileo or *stergein* love may be enough to pull you to the prayer closet. But when the road seems long and is filled with potholes and terrors around every corner, it will be *agape*—breathed into your heart by the Spirit of God—that will charge your prayers with the fearless, relentless, and overpowering demand for victory!

Growing in *agape* love is something we deal with every day if we truly seek God's heart. For some battle-torn families, the struggle means learning to love the unlovely. To those less pressed, this growth may not necessarily be a battleground in their hearts and minds, but it should be a goal.

Whatever your situation, remember that the Holy Spirit, who is *in* you, is the very essence of *agape* love. He alone can produce this valuable fruit, which unfortunately cannot be harvested overnight. So don't grow weary. Relax, and let the Holy Spirit do the work. It will happen in God's timing for you, just as it happened in the life of one of Jesus' disciples.

A DIAMOND IN THE ROUGH

One day, Peter, a young fisherman, met a Man who was to change the course of his life. Like everyone in Israel at that time, Peter felt the ever-pressing concern about Roman tyranny and burdening taxes. As a partner in a fishing business, Peter certainly felt pressured. Otherwise, he lived a normal life; his world centered primarily around family and a small group of friends.

Insignificant as Peter may have been to the rest of the world, in God's eyes he was a diamond in the rough. Reaching out His big eternal arms, God gathered Peter to Himself through Jesus and turned this village fisherman into a fisher of men.

Peter spent the next three years of his life learning new ways, new ideas, and new feelings. His rough exterior gradually gave way to the gentle, caring person on the inside. Peter himself was amazed as he saw values he once held so dear begin to melt. The reality of the far more important eternal values Jesus continually taught soon began to emerge. Being a zealous man, Peter plunged himself into every new challenge Jesus offered. But none of the challenges would be as life-changing as the one yet to come.

The disciples often found themselves caught up in competing with one another. Each believed that none of the others could love Jesus as much or serve Him as faithfully as he. Many of their inferiority feelings came out as superiority attitudes. But one thing was sure: they each loved (*phileo*) Jesus as much as they could. Having given all, they followed Him. Was this not the self-sacrificing love Jesus always talked about? What more could a man give?

At the Last Supper, Peter was almost arrogant in defending himself to the Lord:

> *But Peter said to Him: "Even though all may fall away, yet I will not." And Jesus said to him: "Truly I say to you, that you yourself this very night, before a cock crows twice, shall three times deny Me." But Peter kept saying insistently: "Even if I have to die with You, I will not deny You!" And they all were saying the same thing, too*—Mark 14:29-31 NASB.

Of course, Jesus was correct, and Peter did deny Him. Albeit immediately: *"Peter then went out, and wept bitterly"*—Luke 22:62 (emphasis authors).

AGAPE VS. PHILEO

After His resurrection, Jesus opened up a sensitive conversation with Peter. The Lord tenderly exposed the wounds that would surely scar Peter if not healed by the balm of truth gently applied.

Peter had learned the difference between *phileo* and *agape*. But would his heart bear up under the shame he felt?

Jesus had prepared His disciples a meal on the beach. Unusually quiet throughout dinner, Peter quickly withdrew from the others as soon as they finished eating. His heart was aching, his mind was reeling, and his body was weak from grief. It was too much to bear.

Jesus called to Peter and, motioning toward the others, said: *"Simon son of John, do you truly love [agape] me more than these?"* (John 21:15 NIV).

As Peter looked from Jesus to the others, who were some distance away, his mind raced back to that fateful night when he alone denied Christ—just as Jesus said he would! Peter loved Jesus with every ounce of his strength, but he found that his own strength was no match against Satan's plan to "sift him." (See Luke 22:31.) Pain pierced his heart as he tried desperately to push the memory aside.

Peter fixed his eyes on the Lord's seeking gaze. He knew Jesus was asking: *"Do you love Me with a self-sacrificing love?" The disciple also knew that his only reply could be: "Yes, Lord . . . you know that I love [phileo] you"* (verse 15).

In other words, Peter was saying: "I love You as a friend—my love is limited." As the disciple bowed his head to hide the confusion, Jesus spurred him on: *"Simon son of John, do you truly love [agape] me?"* (John 21:16 NIV).

Peter lifted his tear-filled eyes, again meeting the heart-searching eyes of Jesus. *"Yes, Lord, you know that I love [phileo] you"* (verse 16).

It was as if Peter was saying: "I can't even compete with the others, Lord. I can't say I love You more than they do. We both know the truth. My love for You is weak. I enjoy You and have been consumed with You for over three years; but, obviously, I don't cherish You with my life. I need You, but I'm afraid when You need me. And although I want to be Your most loyal friend, I have found that with my measure of love I will only fail."

In His mercy, Jesus wouldn't stop there. Peter had been brought to some startling realizations about himself in the last several weeks, and it was almost more than his tender heart could bear.

Feeling unworthy and unequipped, he had left the ministry. Jesus knew Peter would be lost to the fishing business forever unless the disciple was brought back into a place of peace and rest, free from tormenting guilt.

A third time the Lord said to Peter: *"Simon son of John, do you love [phileo] me?" (verse 17).*

These words hit like a whip and stung just as badly. Peter broke, and all his grief came gushing out like a cloudburst. The doors between them were now wide open. There were no secret rooms in which to hide. Would Jesus accept his limited love? Yes, Jesus accepted Peter right where he was. Then Jesus said: "Feed my sheep."

Three times during their difficult conversation, the Lord reinstated Peter to the ministry. But it was the following words that told Peter his limited, unsacrificing love would become the greater love he longed to give his Master:

> *I tell you the truth, when you were younger you dressed yourself and went where you wanted; but when you are old you will stretch out your hands, and someone else will dress you and lead you where you do not want to go—John 21:18 NIV.*

Jesus was saying: "I'm going to take your affection and turn it into a love that will cause you to give the greatest sacrifice you could give—the life you sought so hard to protect." Peter would one day possess self-sacrificing *agape* love. And he would learn that this new love never fails.

LOVE'S TRANSFORMING POWER

We can love with less than *agape* love and get through many situations in life. If we are to grow into Christlike maturity, and live the life of the true overcomer. However, we must be willing to exchange our limited capacity to love for Christ's unlimited capacity. Anything less is a love that will eventually fail.

As you can see, little would ever be done in the Kingdom of God if the greatest depth of love we could reach was as weak and shallow as the love Peter originally had. That kind of love is not enough to meet the demands of crises.

Although we may not be faced with life and death situations, we may be faced with crucial circumstances that need love's strong and unyielding care. Are you laboring to keep your family together or to hold a ministry afloat? Perhaps you're weary and frustrated from trying to win a loved one to the Lord. Is your heart battered and worn simply trying to give love the best way you know how, only like Peter, you find it's not enough?

Jesus explained to the disciple that His love would transform. Peter wouldn't have to come to that transformed state in his own power. The same is still true today. The Holy Spirit is still in the business of making weak, selfish people into strong, sensitive people.

In an effort to grasp God's love more clearly and deeply, I began to pray intensely for understanding. Within a few days the Lord gave me a vision of someone I worked with. I'll call her Mary.

As I prayed for Mary, I saw a completely accurate picture. There she stood with a can of beer in hand—stooped shoulders, overweight, with a natural pout on her face. A victim of some unfortunate childhood circumstances, she had become an angry, bitter person. As a result, she was a gossiper—negative and whining.

As Mary stood before me, all of her negative qualities seemed intensified. The Lord told me to love her. "I can't, Lord," was my reply. "I pity her, but I can't love her."

At this point, God began to instruct me in a series of exchanges in my picture of Mary. I was to replace the can of beer with a glass of water, self-hate with self-love, and fear with trust and hope. Peace and a sense of well-being was to replace her deeply rooted anger and bitterness.

Next God directed me to fill her with joy, place an air of expectancy about her future, and watch the depression leave. Suddenly, Mary was surrounded with people who loved her. I could see her loneliness evaporate as she reached out. Love seemed to emanate from her to the people in her world. Changing before my very eyes, Mary lost about fifty pounds and grew two inches as she was standing tall instead of slouching. She was irresistible! Her look of contentment and glee was overwhelming. Then once again came the command to love her. This time I was filled with love for her.

"Lord" I cried: "I do love her. My heart feels like it's going to burst." Then God responded tenderly: "Nita, that's how I love you."

His love is a transforming love. And as the Lord looks at each of His children, He sees them in unqualified perfection. Yet, at the same time He is aware of hurts, scars, and sin in our heart. You say: "How can that be?" Let me explain it like this: although you can't see light, you can see its effects as you walk outside at noon or as you go into a lighted room from a dark hallway. You cannot see the components of light, but that doesn't preclude the fact that they exist. By letting light flow through a prism, its component parts become visible as a beautiful rainbow.

The Holy Spirit acts as a prism in reverse. A fragmented person (sinful man), when seen through the blood of Jesus, is revealed as unified and perfected. God sees both the absolute perfection in which you stand through Christ and the diffused sinfulness with which He must deal. In a prism of love, the Holy Spirit carefully and patiently takes the fractured parts of our fallen nature and makes us whole. The effects of His work become apparent to the world as Christlikeness. We are all being transformed by His relentless love.

GIVING THE TOUCH OF LOVE

Many years ago I was given the opportunity to touch a life with love. Lynn was in her early teens and had experienced many tragedies in her young life that had opened the door to bitterness and rebellion. Drugs, alcohol, and a full-time association with other rebellious teens worked together to lead her down the primrose path of self-destruction.

Lynn's parents were at their wit's end. Although they loved their daughter, they didn't know how to get past her fortress of anger to stop the self-indulgence that would become her ruin.

As I looked at Lynn, I saw a young, confused, and very angry little girl who would need a lot of love, direction, and discipline. While I felt much love and compassion for this teenager, at the same time I was raising a child of my own. Ricci was now old enough to hold tight to the principles I had taught her or to learn from the potentially bad example I was considering bringing into our home. Was I willing to take the risk? Could the love and discipline of our structured environment help Lynn? Could I teach her a new self-love and respect that would transform her life?

Responsibility was something that Lynn eagerly shunned. Would she teach Ricci to shirk and gradually disregard her own training? It seemed like a big risk, but Lynn had opened the door of my heart, climbed into the protective nest that I thought was reserved for moms and their children, and closed the door behind her. It was obvious that she was there to stay—bare feet, blue jeans, halter top, peculiarly braided hair, and all.

As Lynn entered our little family, she brought some ideas with her. From her viewpoint, she would have to retrain us to her lifestyle and openly rebel when she couldn't win by charm or sneak without getting caught.

Ricci, of course, was delighted to have a new big sister in the house, although she didn't understand all these strange people who began to show up whenever Mom wasn't home. Neither could she figure out what those funny little cigarettes were that made everybody laugh. Still, Lynn was the first big sister Ricci had ever had, so she opened her heart and tried to bring this new friend into her world.

On the other hand, I wanted a good life for Lynn. She had been hurt and her values had been distorted. But with effort and encouragement, she would be a happy, shining, *perfect* example of a well-adjusted teenager or so I thought. You might say I wanted to "shine the tarnished brass bowl and make it like new."

It didn't take long to find out something was wrong. Ricci decided she had better tell me what was going on behind my back. With the newly acquired information (now substantiated—it didn't take long once I started looking), I confronted Lynn. With all the love and buffing I was giving my brass pot, I thought it would *want* to shine. She had other ideas. If anyone was going to conform, it would not be her. If we really loved her, we would accept her like she was. Otherwise, she would just leave—which she did!

I felt dazed. How did I fail? I asked myself. This young lady had so much potential. What happened?

In less than a year, I reopened the door to Lynn. By then Lynn's destructive lifestyle had caused her enough pain that she was ready to try again.

This time I decided to take lots of time to get to know Lynn. I wanted to find out where she was coming from and what scars had produced such an angry young lady. The lines of respect were clearly drawn so there would be no questions about our responsibilities toward one another. Ricci was a little older now and this time started out with different expectations. Also, something unexpected had happened to Lynn just hours before she moved in—she had given her life to Jesus Christ.

Transformations came slowly and painfully. I made mistakes, and at times I expected too much too fast. Lynn found herself longing for the carefree days without expectations and responsibilities. Ricci pulled a little too hard on Lynn. But through it all, Lynn had become an intricate and vital part of our family. I could not have loved her more if she had been my own daughter.

I taught Lynn new self-respect—a desire to look ahead and achieve goals. I worked with her and helped dig out the beauties and possibilities I saw in her until she began to see them herself. I praised her every time she made friends who wanted good for their lives and who came from homes established in the Lord. When she gave gestures of kindness to people instead of expecting to receive, I complimented her on her sensitivity. We revamped her wardrobe to fit her new self-image and changed her hairstyle to enhance her pretty face, which now glowed.

During this time, Lynn was engaged to a young man who fought hard to keep her down. But she submitted to my refusal to let them marry until certain conditions had been met by him on a consistent basis for at least a year. My main goal was for her to establish her own self-esteem and turn away from the relationship.

In that period of time, Lynn met someone else—the kind of man I longed to see her marry. Today she is happily married and the mother of four. She and her husband love Jesus.

Lynn is still in the process of healing, changing, and growing. I must admit that it pleases me as much today as it did in the beginning to see each new step of growth. We spent many years laughing, crying, sharing, and growing together. I saw an angry, rebellious, drug-abusing teenager become a beautiful, loving, giving, and compassionate Christ-centered woman—because I took a second chance to give the touch of love.

LOVE COVERS ALL

Peter wrote: *"Above all things have intense and unfailing love for one another, for love covers a multitude of sins"* (1 Peter 4:8 Amplified). I believe this knowledge had etched itself into Peter's mind in a way few of us would ever understand. Christ's love had not only covered his own sin but had poured out its balm of healing on the disciple's wounded heart.

Most people's imperfections can be blinding if we fail to see them through love. As we look at those for whom we are praying, we must train ourselves to see them perfected by love.

The hardest battle we will ever fight in this area will be to *choose* to cover, in love, the person who has broken our trust. It is a choice, however, and one that will turn a proverbial coal mine into a diamond mine if we will let go of our judgments. Love will purge us and heal them when we allow it to reign: *"By mercy and*

*love, truth and fidelity (to God and man, not by sacrificial offerings)
iniquity is purged out of the heart" (Proverbs 16:6 Amplified).*

The Lord isn't interested in our sacrifices or our work to gain
His favor. He is interested in our willingness to love as He loves.
If you choose to cover a person's sin in the balm of love, that sin
will eventually be healed. It is like putting a nice, cool, healing
salve on a burn. You continually pour on the balm of love until
every trace of sin is gone.

That's what God showed me in the vision of Mary when He
first told me to love her. When I couldn't, He let me see what *His
love* would do in her life. Slowly, He poured out His love, healing
and changing each facet of Mary's life until she became a radiant
and beautiful diamond.

I'll never forget the night the Lord spoke to me. I had been
praying into the wee hours of the morning about someone who
was very close to my heart. I longed to help them during their
hours of pain, but I didn't know how my love could possibly help
heal them or turn their world around. I needed the answer, and I
was determined not to quit praying until it came. When at long
last the answer did come, it seemed so obvious that I couldn't
understand why I hadn't seen it myself. The Lord said:

> Nita, love means searching out
> the innermost parts of a person
> until you find the most *wretched*
> thing about them. At that point
> you love them and want their
> well-being enough to *die* for
> them. *Then love cannot fail.*

Agape love expects nothing from the object of its affection, and
it is willing to give its last breath to meet the sincere needs of the
cherished. Love's eyes are not blind to all but the beauty of its
prize, but chooses to cover the flaws with the oil of goodness and
the wine of longsuffering love. Again, we don't ignore faults in

others; but as we see the beauty and preciousness of the loved one, our perspective on their faults change.

When we see them through their "broken love receptacles" getting hurt or hurting someone else—even if it's us—and we realize that we don't have the power to change or fix these "broken receptacles," our love for them forces us to draw from a higher source. It pushes us into prayer to break the power of their damaged reflexive responses and bring God's healing and wisdom to restore them.

POWER THAT BRINGS CHANGE

Prayer yields to us the needed *grace* to "tough it out," so to speak, until victory is ours. Every time we reach for God and let His mercy flow through us to others, a little deposit of mercy falls on our hearts and slowly erodes away the hardness that wants to retaliate; and the hardness is replaced by love.

We can't change people any more than we can take a fish out of water, give it legs and a tail, and say we've changed it into a cat. People have to come to a place where they see the need and develop the *desire* to change. All we can do is release the Holy Spirit to do His ministry in that person's heart to reveal the need and stir the desire to change. This we do through prayer. We ask the Holy Spirit to reveal the nature of *love* to their understanding and give them the desire to love; the *wisdom* to see where they fall short; and the *grace* to believe they can be like Jesus.

In working with Lynn, I fasted and prayed that she could see herself like Jesus sees her—and in so doing, love herself enough to let her old nature and life go so Jesus could dominate her thoughts and ultimately her life. I prayed that God would enlighten me to reflect His love for her and that even in correction she could walk away feeling hope instead of despair.

It was love that drove me to prayer on Lynn's behalf and compelled me to let God change *me* to help her. And it was love that gave me the strength to make sacrifices so she could grow. Love would and still does give me new visions morning by morning for the people in my world. Each new vision graces me with the patience to persevere until the people I love are free and God is glorified.

Gerdie Reidt, daughter of the famous evangelist John G. Lake, was a friend of mine until the Lord recently took her home. One day she related one of her father's amazing experiences.

An angel had appeared to John and spent some time sharing things about the Kingdom. Just before he left, the angel looked at him and said: "John, prayer is the only way into the heart of the Father—one cannot experience the depth of His love except through prayer."

From this angel, John Lake learned the profound truth that you cannot give to another something you have never known yourself. To give Christ's love you must first become acquainted with His love. This you can only do in prayer.

The more you pray, the more absorbed you will become in His love. The more His love fills your heart, the more you will give it to others. The more intimate your relationship with the Lord becomes, the more you'll trust Him. This trust will, in turn, open your heart to give sacrificially and mercifully to others—far beyond your natural human abilities. Having received it from Jesus, you will give it; having given it, you will receive that much more again from Him. Further, as we bring down our defenses and learn to love with the love of Jesus, we grow in understanding His love for us. The scripture encourages us to come to know the depth, length, width and breadth of God's love for us and be filled with this same love to the depths of our innermost being. As we are filled with His love, we love with His love. So, it becomes a means of personal growth that is more precious than gold. Receiving, understanding and giving His love is the means by which we enter into the overcoming life. Through it, we are daily made more perfectly into Christ's image and become the praise of His grace.

The new unswerving trust that will ultimately be developed will cause you to bring the treasures of your heart to rest at His feet, knowing that He *will* complete that good work He has begun.

Chapter 6 —————————————

Humility, A Divine Treasure Chest

One day several years ago, I was sitting by a lake. Nestled high in the Sierra Mountains in California, tranquility and beauty were in perfect harmony. I was there to wait on the Lord for direction for the next year's ministry.

As I looked out over the lake, the Lord began to speak to me in my spirit. He said: "I will teach you about *humility*. I want you to become like water."

"Like water?" I replied.

"Look at the lake and tell Me what you see," He resumed.

Trying hard to understand what God was teaching me, I carefully surveyed the lake and started my list of observations. "Well, the water is crystal clear, and I can see the fish and plant life at the bottom."

"The water is transparent, and so must you be," He affirmed.

"Lord," I said: "I see the sun as it dances on the water."

"As you humble yourself daily, My Son will begin to reflect from you, just as the sunlight reflects off the water."

"Lord," I began again: "I notice that water will form to any shape."

Immediately God said, "So must you be moldable. As you humble yourself, situations and people won't *break* you; but through any difficulty, My Spirit will make you what I want you to be."

I looked around to see if there was more I could learn. Behind me was a waterfall. "Lord, the water seems to delight in rushing to the rocks below."

Again His response came quickly: "This is the heart of humility—don't run to reach the heights of recognition, but humble yourself always and let Me lift you up. That's My law." (See Micah 6:8.)

Again I searched so as not to miss any of His teachings. "I notice that as the wind blows gently, it sends a current rippling across the water."

"When humility has become your way of life, it will take only a gentle blowing of My Spirit to guide you. Pray for humility, and embrace her beauty. As you do, we will become one in heart. All that you ask in secret, I will give you openly. Evil was born in pride—authority over the evil one becomes unlimited in humble submission to My Word. Greatness is found only in the meekness of the Son!"

I pondered the Lord's words for hours. I desired to reach high in prayer and defeat Satan. I wanted to be an intercessor with a heart like Moses and the apostle Paul so that I too, would come to know Christ so well that even my own soul would be of no value compared to the prize of the lost souls and freedom to the saints. (See Romans 9:3 and Exodus 32:32.) I knew that God had given me the precious key to unlock the power of prayer available through Christ.

Humility is the grace that holds within its bosom all other virtues. The fruits of the Spirit are ornaments of grace enshrined in its magnificent beauty. Yet the world is apparently blind to this truth. Humility is like a "divine treasure chest". The bigger the chest, the more treasures within. If your goal is to offer Jesus the greatest "treasure chest" you can possibly give, you will seek each day to walk in greater expanses of "humility." At the end of the journey, when you fall on your face before Christ, you will want to give Him all the glory you heaped up by serving Him faithfully. Many of these treasures will come as a surprise, for you will never know until the end all that has been accomplished through your life. All the treasures given to the majestic "King of kings" will be displayed in the golden treasure chest of humility.

On the other hand, should you choose not to seek after this extraordinary grace, the virtues of His divine nature will be locked away from you, sealed tightly and put against the wall.

How broken you will feel as, one by one His other children honor Him as "Lord of lords" with their overflowing chests of treasures, while the chest with your name on it remains conspicuously unopened and alone. Looking at Him in all His glory, how then could you say: "It was too hard a thing that You asked, Lord"?

THE PRISON OF PRIDE

What is it that can keep us from filling our treasure chests for our King? The answer is simple: *pride*.

We can never experience the freedom of rising high above self, on the wings of *agape* love, while feverishly working to protect self in an impenetrable vacuum of pride and self-justification. One can never flourish in the fruits of the Spirit while making every effort to hide in a cocoon of self-rights and "I'll do it my way" attitudes. On one hand, we try to cultivate humility; on the other hand, pride. They cannot grow together.

In his excellent book, *Humility*, Andrew Murray makes this analogy:

> In an address I heard lately, the speaker said that the blessings of the higher Christian life were often like the objects exposed in a shop window—one could see them clearly and yet could not reach them. If told to stretch out his hand and take, a man would

answer: "I cannot; there is a
thick pane of plate glass between
me and them." Likewise
Christians may clearly see the
blessed promises of perfect peace
and rest, of overflowing love and
joy, of abiding communion and
fruitfulness, yet feel that there is
something in-between hindering
the true possession. And what
might that be? *Nothing but pride.*

Pride is a prison of self-centeredness. The bars holding you in
are self-exaltation, self-glorification self-gratification, and vindication. This results in a constant spirit of striving with God and
man. Unforgiveness, bitterness, and anger are the fruits of pride. I
could go on, but the picture is clear. Pride is a prison, and you are
the victim.

On the other hand, humility is Christ-centered and diametrically opposes self-centeredness. Humility esteems itself small
before God and man. Philippians 2:3 says: *"Let nothing be done
through strife or vainglory; but in lowliness of mind let each esteem other
better than themselves."*

When speaking of humility, the Greeks would say, *poiem ta dika-
ia sigei,* to express its nature. This means "to do habitually the just
and righteous thing in a quiet way unnoticed by others." But this
is only part of the story. God's Word further says:

> *Clothe (apron) yourselves, all of
> you, with humility—as a garb of a
> servant, so that its covering cannot
> possibly be stripped from you, with
> freedom from pride and arro-
> gance—toward one another. For
> God sets Himself against the
> proud—the insolent, the overbear-*

> *ing, the disdainful, the presumptu-*
> *ous, the boastful, and opposes,*
> *frustrates and defeats them—but*
> *gives grace (favor, blessing) to the*
> *humble*—1 Peter 5:5 *Amplified* .

In other words, you can do humble things and not be a humble person. It isn't the act that tells the true story. True humility is born of the Holy Spirit and is the product of His work in you. Your actions, then, become an outgrowth of your inner nature.

The apostle Paul wrote: *"Let this mind be in you, which was also in Christ Jesus" (Philippians 2:5)*. And Jesus said: *"I am meek and lowly in heart" (Matthew 11:29)*. The word "meek" in Greek means: "mild, gentle, and humble" and describes a person who doesn't esteem himself above another. Jesus was saying: "I am mild and gentle, and I don't consider Myself better than you. So come to Me and find My rest." He wasn't asking us to learn a philosophy but rather to adopt a new way of life that would flow from a new heart and a new mind. A mind bathed in the waters of humility is unfettered and has found peace and strength in a harmonious life.

How well I am aware of pride's prison. Several years ago you would have had to search long and hard to find anyone more prideful and self-seeking than I was. As the manager of a real estate office, the broker and I had worked diligently to recruit and train a large sales force. We took one of the smallest real estate offices in my hometown and turned it into one of the most productive residential sales offices in the franchise. In addition, I was one of the top agents, so I had quite a reputation. I believed in getting the job done at any cost. Coupled with skilled organization and a never-take-no-for-an-answer attitude, my success steadily increased.

I was the proud owner of a large, expensive home on the up-and-coming side of town, three cars, rental property, a house full of nice furniture, and a comfortable bank account. It was often said of me, "What Nita wants, Nita gets!"

My younger sister, Valerie, lived with Ricci and me at this time. I was not a Christian, but she had recently become born again and displayed all the zeal of a new believer. Consequently, as I shared my success stories with her, she would always respond with a hearty "praise God!"

On one of these occasions, as I finished telling her about my latest feat, Valerie responded with her usual "praise God," and it grated against me like sandpaper. I jumped up from the sofa, pointed my finger in her face, and shouted: "You will *never* say that in this house again. God is not responsible for my success—*I am!*" With that, I stormed out of the house.

At the time, I had about two million dollars in business, between listings and sales, in my personal portfolio, all of which I lost within *forty-eight hours.* Incidentally, in today's market it would be worth about 6 million. Our office averaged no less than fifteen listings and fifteen sales weekly and usually substantially more, all of which I received an override on. This number of sales and listings fell to two of each the following week. By the third week after my outlandish statement to Valerie, we had no sales or listings. I quit management, and immediately the office business escalated again—but mine did not.

It took only five months to empty my savings and find myself headed for bankruptcy. No matter how hard I tried, I didn't list one property or sell a single piece of real estate during that entire five-month period.

Finally, I told Valerie as I entered the house one day: "I'm locking myself in the bedroom, and I'm not coming out until I find God. I don't want to be disturbed. I won't eat, and I may not sleep; but I'm going to find God." With that, I took a Bible off the shelf, dusted it off, went into my room, and closed the door.

Two days and nights I agonized. I cried, read, repented, and prayed. But I could not figure out how to get Jesus into my heart. I hadn't eaten or slept, and my eyes were so swollen from crying that I couldn't see out of them.

Finally, in desperation, I knelt by the side of my bed and told the Lord: "I know I'm supposed to love the people in my world—but I don't. I know I'm supposed to love my family—but my heart feels dead. The only one I feel capable of loving is my daughter. And I know I'm supposed to love You, Jesus—but I don't. If You really want me to love You and all these other people, You're going to have to do it through me—because unless You do, I can't"!

With that, what seemed like an electrical current of liquid love started at the top of my head, ran all the way down my body, and shot out through my feet. Over and over again this same thing happened, as though I was being washed from the inside out. For ten minutes it continued. When it stopped, I felt so full of love I thought I would explode. I knew Jesus was in my heart!

I got up, ran out to Valerie and Ricci, and hugged them both as hard as I could. Laughing and crying at the same time, I kept saying: "Jesus is in my heart, and I love everybody." They both laughed and cried with me and hugged me just as hard.

That was the beginning. Two months later I received the baptism of the Holy Spirit, and my world turned upside down. I was in love with Jesus. I gave Him the glory for everything and began trying to convert my entire office. God gave me lots of new business, so I didn't lose anything, as I thought I was going to do.

I cut my work hours down to a fourth of what they used to be and spent the extra time in prayer and the Word. I just couldn't get enough of Jesus. Because of my previous reputation, many speaking engagements opened up for me to share my testimony—always with a harvest of souls.

The Lord eventually asked me to give up my material possessions and follow Him. I sold at no profit or gave away everything I had, walking away with three hundred dollars. In that humbled state, I found the true riches of the Kingdom. Twenty years later, I'm more in love with Jesus than ever. My life is dedicated to the Lord's work. For all my victories, I know that my source is the Lord. *Praise God!*

PRIDE VS. HUMILITY

As I sought the Lord about this chapter Jesus appeared to me. I virtually laid at His feet and wept as His own humility and love poured over my soul and he shared the following with me.

In the story of Nabal, David, and Abigail (1 Samuel 25), the Bible provides a magnified look at a prideful heart's devastating actions. In sharp contrast, this drama also gives us a picture of the beauty of humility.

Nabal owned a large ranch outside the village of Carmel in the wilderness of Paran, located just south of Judah. A man of great wealth, Nabal possessed large herds of sheep and goats. Consequently, he employed many ranch hands to aid him in caring for his vast interests.

While some of these men were tending the flocks in the wilderness of Paran, they were met by David and his small army of men. Had David been evil, he could have easily overpowered these vulnerable shepherds and plundered them. Instead, he and his men took the liberty of acting as a wall of defense around them so no harm would come to them or the animals.

David later sent ten of his men to Nabal's ranch to ask for provisions, which by that time had been earned. David had refused to take what he needed by force. Instead, he worked for his supper, so to speak, by protecting Nabal's herds and flocks. Much to their surprise, Nabal's reply was haughty, stingy, and totally ungrateful: *"Who is David and who is the son of Jesse?"* (Nabal could have answered his own question, because he, like all Israel, knew David was their next anointed king.)

Nabal continued: *"There be many servants now a days that break away every man from his master. Shall I then take my bread, and my water, and my flesh that I have killed for my shearers, and give it unto men, whom I know not whence they be?"* (verses 10-11). The very heart of this statement was a lie, for he knew David and his men by their deeds. We see in Nabal's explosive reply that he was wicked, prideful, and foolish. In short, he returned evil for good.

Nabal's only redeeming asset was his wife, Abigail. When she heard her husband's reviling response, her wise heart knew David and his men would slaughter Nabal and his servants. Hurrying to appease this wrath, Abigail loaded up donkeys with generous provisions—two hundred loaves of bread, five dressed sheep, raisins, figs, wine, and five bushels of wheat—and quickly sent them on ahead of her.

Meanwhile, David in his indignation rose up with his six hundred men to retaliate. But before he got very far, he was met with these gifts. A little confused, he stopped to look around. Just then, humility walked up to him; its name was Abigail.

Obviously a woman of beauty, wisdom, sensitivity, and humility, Abigail bowed before David. Then she began to plead for the innocent and offered apologies for her husband's insolence. Telling David to let the Lord deal with her wicked husband and to accept the provisions, she convinced him to let mercy triumph over judgment and avoid needless bloodshed that would later trouble him.

Abigail paid homage to David's position as king of Israel, continually addressing him as lord. In the eyes of man she was a woman of wealth and position, yet she humbly referred to herself as a handmaid. David found himself impressed with her understanding, wisdom, and humility, and it was easy for him to act on her wise counsel.

Conversely, Nabal's arrogance stirred an uproar, not only in David but also in the Lord. The Lord sets Himself against the proud, and He did so with Nabal. As Abigail explained to her husband what she had done concerning the issue with David, fear struck Nabal and paralyzed him. Within ten days he was dead.

God knew that Nabal's attitude toward David was only an indication of his poisoned spirit and wretched heart. In studying Abigail's conversation with David, it is obvious that Nabal had been as cruel to her as to anyone else. His proud, haughty spirit nearly brought death on many innocent people and set the Lord against himself to his own demise. Pride was his destroyer!

When David discovered that God had poured out judgment on Nabal (incidentally, his name means fool), he immediately sent messengers to take Abigail to be his wife. Her response reveals the very nature of the true "bride of Christ." Rather than getting puffed up about becoming David's bride, she said: *"Let thine handmaid be a servant to wash the feet of the servants of my Lord" (verse 41)*. That humble attitude attracted David, and it attracts God, too! First Peter 3:4 says: *"A meek and quiet spirit . . . is in the sight of God of great price."*

THE BLESSINGS OF HUMILITY

This story of David, Nabal, and Abigail depicts profound truths that are extraordinarily beautiful when the Holy Spirit unfolds them for us. We see David as a type of Christ, Nabal as a type of Satan, and Abigail as a type of the Church—the bride of Christ.

Let's briefly retrace Abigail's steps through this dramatic portrayal, in which a multiplicity of emotions are revealed.

Upon hearing what had taken place between Nabal and David, Abigail quickly prepared the provisions for which David had asked. Her first response was to appease his anger. In desperation and fear, she attended to every detail. Perhaps she imagined David with a fierce look—sword drawn and teeth clenched—riding hard to bring destruction, which is probably the way it was. In like manner, God's countenance is fierce toward the proud and defiant. But God is gracious, kind, and adoring toward the humble.

Imagine Abigail's relief when David said: *"May you be blessed"* (*1 Samuel 25:33 NIV*). Jesus said the same thing in His Sermon on the Mount: *"Blessed are the meek" (Matthew 5:5)*. When we come humbly to God, we'll find a rejoicing Savior full of blessing and love, not a mean tyrant with a club.

As already noted, the gifts Abigail gave were really earned by David—just as the gifts of grace we give to our Lord have been earned by *Him!*

It is significant, too, that Abigail was in a hurry to meet David. Perhaps in her quickened pace she stumbled and fell a few times, as saints do today. It's not the number of times we stumble that tells the story, however—it's the number of times we pick ourselves up and continue on course that counts.

Abigail's goal was her future king, and our goal must always be the same. When she found herself standing before David and saw him in the garb of a servant, she was probably surprised. David, no doubt, looked very similar to the other men, just as Jesus came to us clothed in human flesh, looking like any other man. For many, this has been a stumbling block. Philippians 2:7 says Jesus *"made himself of no reputation, and took upon him the form of a servant, and was made in the likeness of men."* He was a servant who washed His disciples' feet!

Abigail appeased David's wrath by offering him what he had earned. Our approach must be in like manner. Don't try to appease God by what you feel *you* have done or earned. Instead come humbly, bearing the gifts of Jesus in you and offering up the good work of Christ in simplicity of heart.

GIFTS FOR THE KING

Each gift that Abigail presented to her king spoke of the King of kings, just as our gifts to Jesus will speak of Him. Abigail gave David two hundred loaves of bread, five dressed (prepared) sheep, two skins of wine, five bushels of roasted grain, one hundred cakes of raisins, and two hundred cakes of pressed figs—all these gifts were loaded on donkeys. For us, "humility" will bear all the virtues we present to Christ. Each one will speak of our majestic King!

The *bread* represents our total dependence on Christ for life. Jesus said: *"I am the bread of life: he that cometh to me shall never hunger."* (John 6:35)

The prepared *sheep* speaks of the completed and perfect sacrifice that Christ, the Lamb of God, was for us. Referring to the atonement needed for the Church, the Bible says: *"With the precious blood of Christ, as of a lamb without blemish and without spot"* (1 Peter 1:19); and: *"He is brought as a lamb to the slaughter"* (Isaiah 53:7). How thankful we are that Christ paid the price! Further, it speaks of the grace of humility that Jesus wroughts in the yeilded heart of His own. It is a grace that beautifully depicts His own nature.

Abigail's gift of *wine* spoke of the precious blood of Jesus that was shed for our sins. Jesus said: *"This is my blood of the New Testament, which is shed for many for the remission of sins"* (Matthew 26:28).

In the *wheat*, we see the whole redemption picture. Jesus spoke of Himself as the grain of wheat. He said to His disciple: *"I say unto you, Except a corn of wheat fall into the ground and die, it abideth alone; but if it die, it bringeth forth much fruit"* (John 12: 24). It was fitting that Abigail, a type of the Church, would send grain ahead of her, a symbol of the abundant fruit birthed by the death of Christ. After His resurrection, Jesus unveiled thousands of grain fields all over the world that were ripe for the harvest, of which we are a part.

The *raisins* represented the divine nature that Christ would bring forth in His bride. (See Galatians 5:22, 23.) These beautiful fruits are a reflection of His glory in the Church.

Finally, the *figs* spoke of the eternal life and its fruitfulness that we, the bride, share with Christ.

All these came to David securely fastened on *donkeys*, the symbol of humility. This both warns and reminds us that all the graces preceding us to Christ will stand arrayed in a golden chest of humility.

As Abigail stood in front of David and his men, she was nervous at first, but that soon gave way to peace. She had come to intercede for the lives of Nabal and his servants; similarly, the Church intercedes for those in bondage to Satan. Abigail found her king tender, responsive, and a joy to be with. As peace flowed over her, she discovered what the Church discovers: true humility is both the essence and the expression of peace with God.

PEACE WITH GOD AND MEN

Have you been struggling through life's problems, burdened with the fear of death? Just as Abigail found peace with David, you can find peace with God. Jesus said: *"Take my yoke upon you, and learn of me; for I am meek and lowly in heart: and ye shall find rest unto your souls. For my yoke is easy, and my burden is light"* (Matthew 11:29, 30).

The Lord is asking for permission to replace Satan's heavy yoke of sin with His own yoke, which is light and brings life and joy. Jesus is meek, He won't ever drive you like Satan does but will gently lead and tenderly care for you. He will be your strength as He develops the beauty of His personality in you. Open the door of your heart, and He will come in and sup with you. (See Revelation 3:20.)

Why not let Him have full control as Lord right now? *You've* been the lord of your own life long enough to discover that you need to turn over full control to Him before you self-destruct. Then you will have peace with God and realize you are the object of His deepest affections.

Open the door of your heart by saying sincerely to Jesus: "Please forgive me. I open the door wide to You. Come and be Lord of my life."

Because Abigail embraced humility, she found favor with the king and his men. All the workers of the land enjoyed her presence. They didn't feel threatened by her. Because she humbled herself before them rather than lifting herself up, they were responsive to her desires. As a result, a great company of men enjoyed peace of mind and heart.

A valuable lesson can be learned here. If you have learned to humble yourself before God, you will humbly serve people. As we saw with Abigail: *"When a man's [woman's] ways please the Lord, he maketh even his [her] enemies to be at peace with him [her]"* (Proverbs 16:7).

What did God find so pleasing about Abigail? Her humbleness of heart!

SPIRITUAL BAROMETERS

I have purposely overlooked an important function that Nabal played. He acted as a *barometer* for Abigail.

We all have a barometer. Each of us has someone in our life who is a pressure gauge, one who exposes the condition of our walk with God. This person may be prized by others, but to you they seem like a stumbling block. It may be your wife, your husband, a child, or a parent. Perhaps it's a relative or the next-door neighbor who likes to spend more time on your doorstep than in their own living room. Whomever it is, you have a choice to make concerning this person and your own walk with the Lord.

Abigail made the right decision. Nabal was obviously a tyrant and could have easily helped create a wretched, squalling wife. Abigail, however chose not to let her well-being rest in his hands. She chose to let the situation make her instead of break her. Responding to his insults with dignity and meekness, which by now were so much a part of her nature, brought her to heights of greatness that Nabal missed—and her king respected.

Abigail knelt at David's feet and asked that Nabal's sin be laid upon her. Only a heart pruned by God, chiseled by trial, and perfected in love and humility could have made such a plea—for her abuser.

Many people have been spiritually, emotionally, and even physically ravished by mean-spirited or morally selfish people. To all the women who have experienced the nearly fatal violation of a husband who has committed adultery; to all of the men who have been equally traumatized by wives guilty of adultery; to all the children who have been nearly destroyed by sexual, physical, or mental abuse; to all the parents who have suffered the shipwreck of rebellious children; and to all those who have suffered through the mutilated self-esteem of being the victim of someone else's abuse and have been able to pick up the pieces of their lives—you have lived out the beauty and freedom of what is portrayed not only in Abigail's life but also in the testimony of the cross—that of the personification of *humility*.

You had to approach the Lord on your knees and say: "Please, Lord, lay their sin upon me so they can be free." In so doing, you chose not to destroy them for what you suffered at their hands. No matter how long it took, you walked out your pain and came to that level of forgiveness.

Few people can resist such love. I could make a list of people who have come to the place of such humble forgiveness— such selflessness—that they have brought their abusers to Christ. Through powerful prayers and living out lives of selfless love, they have been the catalyst for restoration.

Recently, I read an incredible book titled, **Beyond Forgiveness and Church Discipline.** In the story, a pastor and his congregation desired to restore a man who had lived a double life of ministry and sin for years. Although I was impressed with the pastor and his flock, I believe the unsung heroine of the story was the broken man's wife. The pastor, those who stood by him, and the man's wife all took, in essence, the violation of this man's sin upon themselves when they chose to forgive and be instrumental in his restoration.

It was difficult for everyone in the story, including the repentant man. For a man to bear the responsibility of his sin is one thing; but for his mate to suffer the way she did yet choose to put aside her own needs, stay with him, and be a part of the support system of love that helped anchor him in wholeness, was remarkable and worthy of honor. She was a modern day Abigail.

Never gauge your walk with God by the way others respond to you but by the way you respond to others. One man said: "Our thoughts, words and feelings concerning our fellow man are the test of our thoughts, words, and feelings toward God. Our humility before Him is the only power that can always enable us to be humble before others."

True humility is the product of the Holy Spirit in the yielded believer. It takes time to develop. Your attitudes toward unlovely people and unpleasant situations, however, will help shape the eventual outcome of you as a person.

In his book, *Humility*, Andrew Murray writes:

> *If once we learn that to be nothing before God is the glory of man, the spirit of Jesus, the joy of heaven, we will welcome with our whole heart the discipline we may have in serving even those who try to vex us. When our own heart is set upon this, the true sanctification, we will study each word of Jesus on humility with new zest, and no place will be too low. No stooping will be too deep, and no service too mean or too long continued, if we may but share and prove the fellowship with Him who spoke, "I am among you as he that serveth"* (Luke 22:27).

Nabal was an oppressive force in Abigail's life, yet she kept her heart pure. As a result, she became a powerful vessel adorned with the graces of the Spirit fit for the Master's use. This should be our goal in every similar situation.

The life of the overcomer is one graced in the resplendent virtue of humility. It is a grace that is most highly prized by all of heaven and most importantly of all, by Christ who has Himself shown us the great value of this virtue. As we continually walk in voluntary humility, God is able to add to our effort the gift of His own humility, thus bringing us to maturity. When all is said and done, we, like Abigail, will be called away by our King. Our first reaction will be as hers was—to bow before Him and pay homage to the One who bought our souls. Every word spoken will be in depths of humility never reached here on earth. He will say to rise as He begins to speak to us—but how do you stand before One so great as God? Yet, even then, in the greatest moments, will come the supreme unveiling.

As Nabal was judged by God for his wretchedness, Satan, too, will be struck by the Lord. Like Nabal, who grieved all those around him, Satan, too, will meet his bitter end in the lake of fire prepared for him. But we will remember his cruelty no more as we are held eternally in the loving arms of our Savior and Lord.

Just as David sent his servants to claim Abigail as his wife, Jesus will send the Holy Spirit on a special mission to gather His Church. As we are caught up to meet our Husband in the sky, all that remains of this world will pass away.

First Abigail met David, a king in servant's garb. When he came into his kingdom, he claimed her as wife. Even then the whole picture was not revealed. She saw herself as a servant of her king's servants. It wasn't until she met him face to face that the reality of the promise was revealed.

Nor will the complete reality or our position be known until that great day. With our eyes fixed on our *King,* we will wait until at last the veil is forever removed. There we will stand, adorned in our wedding gown as beautiful and bright shining as the sun. As we stand face to face with our Jesus, we, the bride, will know Him as we are known. Overwhelmed and carried away by His great love, we will become perfectly and eternally united with our blessed Husband.

Chapter 7 ————————————

Seasons Of Growth

As I was seeking the Lord about how to present this chapter, He gave me a vision of a piece of transparent fruit; inside I could see a little seed. Then He spoke to my heart and said: "The seed of life is in the fruit."

The answer to our prayers—the harvest—is wrapped up in the fruit of the Spirit. This isn't to say you must bear perfect fruit if you want answers to prayer. What you will discover, however, is that life in Christ itself becomes a prayer and will bring forth the answers to many of your heart's desires.

The apostle Paul writes in *Galatians 5:22-23: "The fruit of the Spirit is love, joy, peace, longsuffering, gentleness, goodness, faith, meekness, temperance: against such there is no law."* Let's look at how these fruits develop and will ultimately produce answered prayer.

SEASONS OF STILLNESS

The Bible says all of nature speaks of God. (See Psalm 19:1-6, Romans 1:19, 20.) Not only does it show forth His handiwork, but it also speaks of His ways. For instance, we can look at a fruit-producing tree and see a perfect picture of how the Holy Spirit works in you and me.

First, a seed is planted in the soil, just as we were planted in Jesus. But then an interesting thing happens. The seed dies and would seem of no value to the soil. The soil's greatest value at this time is in housing the seed as it remains in the vulnerable state. In the Word, we learn of this same principle in the life of a saint:

> *All of us who have been baptized into Christ Jesus have been baptized into His death…. For if we have become united with Him in the likeness of His death, certainly we shall be also in the likeness of His resurrection—Romans 6:3,5 NASB.*

The word "baptism" represents not only a natural public baptism but, more importantly, a spiritual baptism into the Body of Christ. When we are buried (or planted) with Him through baptism, we die.

I call this phenomenon the "season of stillness." To you and the world, your new life in Him seems hidden. As you read the Word, it sinks into the seedbed of your heart and apparently lies dormant. Although you pray, you're sure the Lord must be upset with you because the heavens seem like brass. While others around you are flourishing, everything in your spiritual life seems dead. People in your world are positive you have backslidden. You're pretty sure you have, too, but you can't figure out how it happened.

A pastor in Selma, California, told me a story about one of the new members of his congregation. Apparently, the man's wife had been a faithful member for well over a year when her husband suddenly started coming to church. After about four months, the pastor decided to invite this man out to lunch. After four months of altar calls, the pastor was concerned as to why this man hadn't accepted the Lord as his Savior. The man's wife was equally perplexed.

Sitting at the table in the restaurant, the pastor plowed right in. "Ben, you have been faithful in your attendance at church, but I'm concerned about the condition of your soul. Is there any reason why you wouldn't like to make Jesus the Lord of your life?"

Ben looked shocked, then sad. "Pastor," he said: "I already have."

The pastor was dumfounded. "Why haven't you told anyone—at least your wife?"

Ben looked rather solemnly into the pastor's eyes and said: "Well, I just wanted my life to show it. I didn't feel it was something to brag about. I just wanted my commitment to show in the way my life changed. But I have to admit," he said reluctantly: "I've been very disappointed that no one can tell—not even my wife. Why, I heard her just last night praying for my salvation. What should I do?"

The pastor couldn't help but grin as he explained that Ben's plight was typical. He encouraged Ben to make a public confession and promised that with the Body's help, the power of the Holy Spirit, and encouragement from his wife, the changes would soon be apparent enough. Ben would soon spring forth in new life. So will you.

You died with Christ and now live in Him. All your questions and confusion will soon come into fruitful understanding.

A SEASON OF CHANGE

Although you are securely planted in the Holy Spirit, there has not yet been a true *identification* with His personality and character. That takes time. Only seasons with the Lord give birth to this identification. When your dormant "season of stillness" finally ends, it gives way to new life. The signs of such a change are clear: the seed begins to open and struggle through the ground, sending out roots to establish its life-support system; and a tiny stem rises that will one day be a sturdy trunk.

This is a time when you as a new Christian are experiencing the movement of the Holy Spirit as He begins stirring within your innermost nature. He is taking hold, causing a desire in you, His precious child, to know and become more like your Lord. Old friends can see a difference in you as you hungrily respond to the movement of the Holy Spirit in your heart—but perhaps not yet enough to convict them of their own sin.

Just as a little plant pushes out of the ground and reveals its new life to the world, you as a young Christian are bearing significant but small signs of your new nature to your world around you. It is precious to see this new life almost smile with wonder as it opens its new leaves to drink in the rain and bask in the sun.

What we *can't* see, however, is the way the seedling sends out roots deeper and deeper into the soil, claiming territory and causing its new home to respond to its need, while at the same time producing value in the soil.

During this time, Jesus is working in a much deeper way in your life. The roots of your new nature are reaching out and claiming territory in the human nature. The yearning of your soul is becoming dominated by the desire to be one with the Christ who has become your new home.

In this changing season, the world sees a new look of wonder in you. As you grow more dependent on the Lord and less dependent on the world for your sense of well-being, a new strength starts to develop through all kinds of weather. Although this is a very vulnerable time for you as the Lord's young seedling, He gives His special attention to the nurturing and growth needed for strong and fruitful development.

It was during this time of growth in my sister Valerie's life that I found myself perplexed. All she talked about was Jesus. She took her Bible everywhere and seemed to have some reason to go to church every night. Concerned over my baby sister's zeal, I went to talk with our pastor, Dale McNeil.

Dale's secretary had just poured us both a cup of coffee when I shared that I was afraid that Valerie had become a . . . Jesus freak! Dale had just taken a drink of coffee, which he immediately sprayed all over his desk—as he bellowed in laughter.

As my pastor cleaned the mess on his desk, he explained to me that Valerie had been baptized in the Holy Spirit and that her zeal was wonderfully normal. She was like a child with a new friend. "Give her time, and wisdom will come," he assured me. "She won't end up on Haight-Ashbury as a flower child." With that, he introduced me to Valerie's experience and a new step of growth in my own life.

COMING INTO FULL BLOOM

As a tree continues to grow, the nature of the seedling becomes more apparent. Its trunk grows stronger and its foliage becomes thicker and more plush. It provides a resting place for the birds of the air, shade for the beasts of the field, and protection for younger and weaker trees.

This represents a new season for you as a child of God. The Christ-nature now dominates over your old sinful nature. You may not see much fruit yet, but the signs of abundance are on the branches. The things you say and do are lush with the attributes of our Lord. Your life has taken on the characteristics of the kingdom of light, and the world sees Jesus as *He* is unveiled through your life. People in your world find confidence in your strength and look at the Christ in you for shelter from the storms that beat so relentlessly.

Some friends of mine, Ted and Susy, have encountered many and various types of storms. At one point Susy made the statement to me over lunch that she was concerned that people see them as failures because of all their trials.

Many of our mutual acquaintances had said just the opposite. Few could understand how Ted and Susy could stand so strong and still reach out to be a shelter for others while they themselves were going through so much. Without fail, those who mentioned them did so in admiration and respect. I hold them out as precious testimonies of real people becoming Christlike at any price.

As growth continues, spring arrives, and the flowers bloom. A tree is never more lovely than when it is in full bloom. All the world stops to enjoy its wonderful fragrance and revel in the expression of its beauty.

So it goes with you and me. This is a season of great favor. Winter storms have passed, and life has taken on a new look. There is a refreshing at hand. Those in the world who seek this beauty will stop and receive the sweet aroma of Jesus, who has bloomed in and through you.

What a tranquil picture you will afford to those who are weary—an expression of hope and an invitation to new life. You will stand as an example of great expectation and rare beauty to a hurting, tarnished world. They will want your beauty and long to take it home with them. You'll be at rest, delighting in the privilege of reflecting the delicate and picturesque loveliness of Jesus. Every smell of His fragrance is healing for those who draw near.

BEARING FRUIT

As spring flowers give way to a rich yield of fruit, the tree takes on a succulence. Tiny fruit pushes forth, swells, and ripens, and the tree has now realized its purpose for being. Those who pass by are tantalized by its fruit and naturally respond by picking and eating these delectables.

The Holy Spirit excitedly awaits this day in the life of a yielded believer. The Bible says: God "works in you and accomplishes that which is pleasing in His sight, through Jesus Christ, the Messiah" (Hebrews 13:21 Amplified). He has worked His divine work in you to produce the beautiful and vital fruit of the Spirit.

None of the many different seasons you will go through in your walk with the Lord are as exciting as this one. Those in your world are by now being powerfully affected by the Christ-life you display. You are a tree firmly planted by the water, drinking the life-giving water of the Holy Spirit through prayer and the Word. You are not only producing shade for the weary, but fruits of grace that will restore and transform their world.

My dear friend Beverly, is a pastor's wife and the mother of two fine children. I recently spent some time in their home. As always, I marveled at the transparent and sensitive nature of this wonderful lady. She was going through one of the most difficult times of her life, yet she portrayed a strength and loveliness that only maturity in Christ can bring.

Beverly's phone rings constantly as people reach out to someone they know can always be depended upon. I've watched Beverly turn, quietly and sincerely, in a split second from her own pain to reach out to someone in need. Her poised and gracious manner can uplift the most storm-struck soul and send them off in new confidence and inspiration. How I value Beverly, a precious gift to the Body of Christ.

The Lord tells us in His Word that He desires that we may *"abound in and be filled with the fruits of righteousness which come through Jesus Christ, the Anointed One, to the honor and praise of God—that His glory may be both manifested and recognized"* (Philippians 1:11 Amplified).

Again, the fruits of the Spirit are love, joy, peace, longsuffering, gentleness, goodness, faith, meekness, and temperance. These are not fruits of our human nature and can be produced only by the nature of Christ effectually working in us.

Just as a tree must have soil in order to survive, we must stay firmly rooted in Christ if we are to come to the maturity He desires of us. How? By maintaining a Word-and-prayer life. The rest of the work of producing the fruit is the "work of the Spirit." This is clearly expressed by our Lord in John 15.

As I stated in the beginning of this chapter, "the seed of life is in the fruit." *Christ is the seed of life,* or, as Peter put it, the "incorruptible seed." (See 1 Peter 1:23.) Jesus is wrapped in the bosom of the fruit of the Spirit. Each time someone partakes of the fruit of your branches, therefore, he or she is partaking of the life-giving Christ.

HARVESTING YOUR PRAYERS

You may have some long-standing prayer requests that seem virtually impossible. Think about some of those prayers now. Imagine the people you are praying for responding to the fruit of Christ as I share some examples.

My younger sister, Valerie, and her husband, Doug, have a deep burden for souls and have helped lead many into God's Kingdom. I asked a few of these precious people what they saw in Doug and Val that made them want Jesus. In every case, the answer was *joy*. My daughter and I were both powerfully influenced by Valerie's joy. Only the Lord could say how much her joy was responsible for Ricci and me coming to the saving knowledge of the Lord Jesus.

I have mentioned my friend Melinda. Her mother was much used by the Lord to start charismatic prayer groups throughout the San Juaquin Valley during the Catholic charismatic renewal in the 1970s. I have seen her lead people to Jesus. As she talks to them, a river of love seems to flow from her and enfold the one to whom she's witnessing, until in tears they accept Jesus as Lord.

Bearing fruit is not always easy at first. A friend of mine, Jane, accepted Jesus as her Savior and, as a result, was bitterly persecuted by her co-workers. She stayed and prayed. After one year, the Lord released Jane to change positions. Within two months, she was given the opportunity to lead a woman from her old office to the Lord.

When I asked this new Christian what she saw in Jane that made her want Jesus, she quickly responded: "Her long-suffering. No matter what people did or said, she didn't change. She continued to do kind things for them. This wasn't her nature before she accepted Christ." The fruit of Jane's new nature helped someone else find saving grace in Christ.

Jesus said: *"Herein is my Father glorified, that ye bear much fruit; so shall ye be my disciples."* (John 15:8) We must bear quality fruit to meet the demands of successful living on this earth.

Patience ensures that you won't grow weary in well-doing. Every harvest takes time. *Joy* holds you in strength as you work the fields set before you; and it draws others to you instead of pushing them away. *Peace* shelters you in its divine standard. When the enemy comes in like a flood, you will be unmoved by circumstances.

I can still vividly remember a traumatic time in my brother's life. He had been staying with my mother for a few weeks when I noticed a change coming over him. "Dale," I said: "you seem more at rest than I've seen you in a long time. What is it that you see in Mom that's helping you so?"

He uttered only one word: "Peace."

Meekness gives you the Christ-vision of seeing every soul of equal value to your own. Who can run from a servant's heart like that?

Walking adorned with the fruits of the Spirit is in reality walking in God's wisdom; and it gives birth to the fruits of our labor. Just as an apple carries within it seeds that will give life to more apple trees, you carry the ability to create new life inside the fruit you bear—the answers to your prayers, and your life as an overcomer.

THE PURPOSE OF TRIALS

We have spoken about the beauty of the fruit and its development, but we haven't talked about the *destructive* power of the fruit of the Spirit.

Does that statement surprise you? Think about it. The fruit of the Spirit become innate weapons of our warfare. When someone hates you or is indifferent to you, yet you shower them with love, you destroy the work of evil. When joy released destroys the work of depression, Satan is driven away. When the person for whom you're praying bombards you with insults and heart-wrenching criticism, yet you respond in meekness and remain faithful in your intercession, you can only win. Satan will lose.

Every time you exercise the fruits of the Spirit and release their power, it is like dropping a hand grenade in the enemy's foxhole. It is that powerful.

Jesus prayed to the *Father*: "*I do not ask that You will take them out of the world.... Just as You sent Me into the world, I also have sent them into the world*" (John 17:15, 18 Amplified).

Then He said to His disciples: "*In the world you have tribulation and trials and distress and frustration*" (John 16:33 Amplified).

Jesus' words sum up the real world! He never promised we would escape these things. What the Word does promise is this: "*Greater is he that is in you, than he that is in the world*" (l John 4:4); and "*Be of good cheer; I have overcome the world*" (John 16:33).

The first thing you need to do is relax. If your life isn't trial-free, don't be angry with yourself or think you're a failure as a Christian. One of the wonderful things about Jesus is that He teaches each of His own how to rise above problems. We need to realize that the *problem* is not the true problem; it's how we handle the problem—that is the problem.

As we search the Scriptures daily and spend time in prayer, the Lord will make His wisdom known to us. Then we will begin to see each trial through the eyes of victory, perceiving it as an opportunity to enlarge the harvest of fruits on our branches and wield chaos and destruction to the devil's kingdom.

Let me show you the Lord's workings in bringing forth His fruit through trials in the beautiful poetry of the *Song of Solomon*. The Shulammite woman prayed:

> O, I pray the cold north wind and
> the soft south to blow upon my gar-
> den, that its spices may flow out [in
> abundance for you in whom my
> soul delights]. Let my beloved come
> into his garden and eat its choicest
> fruits—Song of Songs 4:16
> Amplified .

The cold north wind speaks of adversity. I'm not suggesting you pray for adversity, for Satan will offer enough of that on his own. But we should never be afraid of troubled times. If we press into the Lord, difficulties will make us *strong*. As the cold north wind blows on the fruit tree, the adverse conditions cause its roots to reach deep into the earth and its trunk to grow in strength as it withstands nature's unfavorable conditions. So it is with us. When trial produces the delectable fruit of patience, you are not only pleasing to the Lord but a wonderful testimony to others. The Lord would never allow trials to destroy us. Instead, He wants to show what good there is in His beloved children and to bring to light those highly-esteemed fruits. If destruction comes, it is because of our bad decisions not the Lord's failure.

THE HEAVENLY GARDENER

My sister Marci was a gem from the beginning. She seemed to be the center around which our family turned—the inner wheel that held the spokes in place. Like the rest of us, I have always marveled at the depth of her ability to love when anyone else would have quit.

Marci reached out many years ago to help two little girls go through an outrageous court case. These children had been molested by their father. Their own mother stood against them as the agonizing trial continued. Marci alone stood like a concrete pillar to protect those children from the very legal system that had the power of their future in its hands.

How I admired her determination to protect those girls at any cost. How I wept and longed for her peace as the fury of hell buffeted her life.

As the years went by, I saw a strong, vivacious woman, who had spent most of her life *giving*, broken. Nine years of battle left Marci weary and battered. But she belonged to God, and God would not forsake her. I stormed heaven in prayer and fasting for the Lord's peace and restoration to come to my dear, sweet sister.

Feeling angry, defeated, even deserted by God, Marci sought refuge and a renewed life. The storm had claimed nearly everything she held dear. But she won. As though overnight, the sun arose, a new day began, and she experienced God's healing and restoration along with a new freedom in love and a new dimension in God. The family began to see the old Marci reappear—this time, however, with a new strength and a growing wisdom.

Marci had hit bottom only to find her Rock—Jesus Christ. From that point, she began to rebuild her life, growing faster and stronger, with a new zeal to reach out and let the Christ in her flow out to hurting people.

The Lord loves showing off to the world and the spiritual realm the value that He sees in you. Jesus is showing Marci off. He used her to save two little girls from a life of disaster. Someday, as she and her husband continue to prepare for ministry, He will show her *love* to a lost and dying world.

The Shulammite woman asked for the warm south wind. When Marci was in the midst of her despair, she too, cried out for the warm south wind to blow over her life. This is the wind of favor, which brings comfort, joy, and rest. But it is not the season in which the child of God grows.

Peter loved Jesus and wanted Him with his whole heart; but it took a tumultuous storm to discover that he had the strength to believe Jesus for the miracle of walking on the water. These sweet times of tranquil favor bring healing to the soul. They rebuild courage and revitalize stamina; but we must never stop there.

The mature fruit of the Spirit will cause you to dwell in harmony with God and man, regardless of situations around you. They are birthed during the hour of adversity—*if* we do it God's way.

When the fruits are lush and ripe in a Christians life, he has reached a grand pinnacle of maturity. This is a place in God that can only be reached in prayer. In all seasons of growth, a life of prayer remains the essence that makes growth possible and develops the well rounded life of beautiful Christlikeness. Without prayer the tree will never much grow. With it the tree will come to bear the glory destined by the Lord for the overcomers alone.

The Shulammite woman then said: "Let my beloved come into his garden and eat of its choicest fruits." We see here a maturity of experience and knowledge in the young maiden.

She has learned that if she will let her heavenly Gardener have His way, she will in time be able to offer up to Him the choicest fruits of love, joy, peace, longsuffering, gentleness, goodness, faith, meekness, and temperance.

The Christ-fruits are our glory. It is the Heavenly Gardener who enjoys the beauty of His labor as He beholds the glory He has produced on the branch. His heart dances as He partakes of this delectable fruit.

Jesus is blessed every time a child of God bears fruit for His Kingdom. As you grow in grace and begin to exhibit the fruits of the Spirit, you will bring joy to the Lord, who will in turn shower you with more grace and cause more growth—thus you will exist in a continuous circle of blessed growth and giving in your relationship with the Lord.

It is prayer that nurtures the tree in every season, thereby developing the fruit—and the fruit nurtures all components of the Christ nature that ultimately develop the prayer.

Chapter 8 ───────────

The Gift Of Obedience

One spring morning as I gazed out my large picture window, I sat entranced at the scene unfolding before me. The surface of the lake was rippled from the geese that had flown down to engage in some fishing. Fish jumped here and there in gay merriment, teasing their approaching predators.

Surrounding the lake were lush trees, their branches adorned with the life of spring. Two birds busily constructed their nest amidst this array of leafy protection, while others filled the air with singing. The crisp, blue sky was smattered with big billowy clouds perfectly poised. Flowers of every color bloomed throughout the scene.

The more I scanned the awesome beauty of God's creation, the more I could feel my heart bursting with love for Him. Finally, I became so full I exploded with praise! With tears streaming, I cried: "I love You, Lord——so much that there aren't words in any language to express how I feel." I will never forget His reply, which sounded gently in my heart: "Nita, when there aren't enough words to say I love you, *obedience* says it all."

In that moment my heart longed to be obedient to Him more than anything I could ever want in my life.

Recalling that moment now makes me think of another time, another place, and another person. The time—the beginning of man; the place—the garden of Eden; the person—Adam.

GIFTS IN THE GARDEN

Adam was in the midst of discovery about himself and the dazzling world around him. He had been given the beautiful birds, lovely butterflies, and animals of every kind, shape, and size. All were gifts from the Father. How often he must have exploded into heights of joy as he partook of the resplendent colors surrounding him. Nature was in perfect harmony, and Adam knew only peace and joy.

I can see the Lord coming to Adam in the middle of the day— His heart brimming with love. "Adam," the Lord would say: "I was thinking about you today, and I thought it would be fun to bring you some presents. Look what I have for you." In a split-second, Adam found himself surrounded by animals of all shapes and sizes, Many of these he had already seen, but many were still new to him.

"What in the world are these creatures?" Adam asked in amazement.

Laughing, the Lord replied: "That's for you to decide. You're free to call each one whatever you desire. Whatever you name them is what they will be called from now on." Then the Lord escorted him from one animal to another.

"Look at this one, Adam. As you can see, it is a very gentle creature—you can see it in his eyes. Notice the spots on the little one's back and the antlers on the male. What will you call these, Adam?"

"Oh, they are exquisite", he replied. "I don't know why, but they remind me of You. I'll call them 'deer' as a memorial to You, Lord, because You are dear to me."

The Lord then led Adam to animals too numerous to mention. Finally, He brought Adam to a snow-white creature that looked more like a cloud of cotton than an animal.

"Adam," the Lord began: "someday this animal will play a vital role in the economy of things. As I look at it, I'm reminded of My great love for you. It will stand as a constant reminder of that love." Then, stroking the gentle animal, He turned to Adam and said: "Someday you'll understand My words. What will you call it?"

"Lord, I'm humbled by this gift, yet my heart is full of joy as I look at him. I want to call this one a 'lamb.' Would that please You, Father?"

The Lord then smiled as He led Adam to the birds, butterflies, and insects—then to the sea to scan its depths and gaze at the wonders of the fish and plant life it housed.

As the Lord turned to leave, He looked back at Adam and said: "If you want or need anything, just speak to Me in your heart, and I will hear."

THE DAY GOD CRIED

It wasn't long before Adam found himself longing for a companion. He didn't really understand his own longing. But, God could hear his heart. He put Adam to sleep and gave him Eve. Now this was a new kind of joy Adam hadn't felt before. But oh! How his love for the Creator grew through this gift. Life was truly paradise. What more could a man ever want than peace and harmony with his God, his wife, and all creation? Nothing could ruin the wonder of it all.

It wasn't long, however, before Adam learned another truth. We know too well that Adam and Eve fell prey to temptation. As he stood before his wife, who held the forbidden fruit in her hand, Adam knew what was happening. That fruit was as peculiar to the garden as an apple in a bucket of oranges. I can imagine the Spirit of God quickening to Adam: *"Don't eat it."*

Adam's mind must have been reeling as Eve told him what the serpent had said. "But, Adam, it said the fruit would make us like God. We won't die; but we will ascend to be as God." His heart was beating rapidly, and his mind was spinning. Would God lie to me? Isn't what we have enough? I told Him I'd never disobey! Would God cheat me? How can this be true?

Looking intently at Eve, his eyes piercing, Adam glanced at the fruit and, without another thought, took it and ate.

Immediately, he felt the effect. Adam looked first at his fallen wife and then at himself. The light that had shown from them so brightly was gone. He looked all around and realized that everything had changed. The birds had stopped singing, and the animals were no longer playing. The silence was deafening.

Something quickly made Adam frightened and insecure. "That *presence*, is gone!" Spontaneously, he took Eve's hand and began to run. "God is not with us, Eve. We have to hide."

In the cool of the day, God came into the garden and found the frightened couple. They responded to His call for the first time in fear and trembling, and Adam explained what had happened. God listened! Then with deep pain in His eyes, He slayed the lamb that Adam himself had cherished and prepared garments for them to wear.

Then He quietly shared with them the things that would come as a result of their blatant disobedience. He explained why they would now have to leave the garden and live in a world of pain and agony.

Adam saw a very calm God that day. But what he didn't know was that God had been watching while he and Eve conversed about the willful act of disobedience. As Adam's mind went back and forth trying to decide what to do, God was pleading, *Don't do it!* As Adam ate the fruit and all creation fell, God looked down through eternity and saw all His precious children who would follow Adam and Eve in sin, so many ending in the portals of hell. Knowing He could never again commune with them and hold them close as He once had, He felt the spear pierce His side, the blood pour from His brow, and the nails drive through His hands and feet. As the stark reality of His loss hit Him, *God cried!*

As Adam and Eve left Eden, God called the cherubim to guard the tree of life. Turning as He watched His children leave His presence, God knelt down and, with His heart breaking, wept.

VICTORY IN THE GARDEN

We are still living in the aftermath of that one act of disobedience today. But God made a stream in the desert and a way in the wilderness. His tears were not in vain.

There came to us another Adam. This man was from Galilee, and His name was Jesus—fully man and fully God, He called us to come to the Father through Himself and promised that He would show the way.

Jesus Christ faced every temptation known to man, yet He proved victorious. He said: *"If you love me, obey me."* (See John 14:15.) He knew His own commitment of love to the Father and to man. How well He knew of the fatal consequences of disobedience. He could see all too clearly how the human race had taken on the barbaric and habitually sinful nature of their self-appointed head, Satan. Yet, God yearned to restore His children to a life of peace and joy dominated by love rather than hate and fear.

Jesus came to redeem us and show us what a life of obedience to God could be like. We felt His love; we heard His wisdom; and we saw His grace and beauty. We saw how Jesus walked so closely to the Father, not fearing man but seeking His glory only from God. We saw His power over evil and the liberty He brought to all who were held captive in body, mind, and soul. And we saw the effects of a life committed to perfect obedience to the Father.

Jesus' obedience was to be tried to the utmost, for the prize lay on the other side of the veil of death. All that He had suffered in His obedience could not be compared to what it would take to tear open the veil. Looking intently at His disciples, Jesus remarked:

> *I have come to cast fire upon the earth, and how I wish that it were already kindled! I have a baptism with which to be baptized, and how greatly and sorely I am urged— impelled, constrained— until it is accomplished—Luke 12:49, 50 Amplified .*

The cup of obedience was not nearly filled. When all else had been said and done, it was time to prepare for final victory. Jesus raised His voice amid the crowd:

> *Now My soul is troubled and distressed, and what shall I say? Father, save Me from this hour [of trial and agony]? But it was for this very purpose that I have come to this hour [that I might undergo it]. [Rather, I will say] Father, glorify—honor and extol—Your own name—John 12:27, 28 Amplified.*

As the hour of tortuous grief drew nearer, the agony began to mount. After having been with His disciples, Jesus entered the garden. It was in a garden that it all began, and would be in a garden that it would end.

So great was Jesus' agony in prayer, so terrible the battle, that heaven sent an angel to strengthen Him. Yet the battle raged in ever-increasing dimensions until Christ's own body could no longer bear the torture.

Still Jesus prayed. He fought. He agonized. He held victory by the horns and refused to let it go. Jesus' sweat became great drops of blood, and His body pushed beyond its limits of endurance; death was imminent. Yet never did He once pray, Father help Me be obedient. *Disobedience was never a consideration.*

The victory was manifested at Calvary, but it was won in the garden—the very place it was lost thousands of years ago.

When Christ rose from prayer, weary and only hours from death, He was confident of His victory. Holding the prize in His bosom, He would endure the cross for the joy set before Him. (See Hebrews 12:2.)

HOW CAN WE OBEY GOD?

Because Jesus *obeyed* with His life, we now live again in Him. Christ was the greatest intercessor known to man. There will never be His equal. Indeed, there will never need to be. This, however, is the point Jesus made with His word and His life:

> *If you [really] love Me you will keep (obey) My commands—John 14:15 Amplified .*

> *If any one would serve Me, he must continue to follow Me . . . conform wholly to My example, in living and if need be in dying— and wherever I am, there will My servant be also—John 12:26 Amplified .*

Obedience is the key to being Jesus' servant. He didn't say: "Where my servant is there will I be," but rather: "Where I am there will my servant be." He leads; we follow. The great intercessors have all learned this valuable lesson many times in their lives.

We have been given the sonship that Adam lost in the fall and Christ regained in His ascension: *"The Spirit Himself bears witness with our spirit that we are children of God"* (Romans 8:16 NASB). *(See also Ephesians 1:20.)* He was raised to be seated at the Father's own right hand, thereby conferring on us the Spirit of sonship. Lifting us to be seated with Him in heavenly places as sons, we are therefore heirs of Christ and His eternal knowledge, wisdom, prudence, riches, majesty, glory, honor, power, might, and dominion. (See Ephesians 2:6.)

Not that we are equal to Christ—He is still God, the great I AM. We are saints, God's inheritance through Christ. But now we are sons, once again having access to the garden and tree of life through Christ.

The word "son," found in Galatians and Romans, is, in the Greek, *huios*. It means "adult son." *Huios* not only speaks of the relationship we have with the Father, but in its original sense also expresses the Father's innate qualities inherent in His Son. Although we still have the inherent qualities of our sinful nature just as we did when we were sons of perpetual disobedience, we also have a new nature. (See Ephesians 2:2.) Our new nature is to obey, not to disobey. So what, you may ask, is the trigger that will cause us to respond to Christ in obedience?

Love is the horse that draws the cart of obedience. The more you love God, the more you'll desire to obey Him. On the other hand, the more you obey Him, the deeper your love and appreciation for Him will grow. Love and obedience go hand in hand.

Jesus said: *"This is eternal life, that they might know [ginosko] thee the only true God, and Jesus Christ, whom thou has sent"* (John 17:3).

Ginosko means to have an experiential knowledge. We must experience His love, faithfulness, and mercy if we are to trust Him. Then we will be as readily obedient to His every desire as Jesus was.

A MATTER OF LIFE AND DEATH

The apostle Paul was an excellent example of what God's transforming love will do. Born into wealth and position, he turned from it all and chose for the sake of Christ to become, as he called himself, a "bondslave." Living without most creature comforts to serve his King, Paul was beaten, whipped, stoned, and even left for dead on a few occasions. Why? He wrote in his letter to the Galatian church:

> *I bear on my body the brand marks*
> *of the Lord Jesus, [the wounds,*
> *scars and other outward evidence of*
> *persecutions]—These testify to His*
> *ownership of me!—Galatians 6:17*
> *Amplified.*

Paul knew and honored the Lord ("Despot") of his life. The word "despot" in the New Testament is the same as *adonai* of the old. Both mean "master." If Christ is our Master, we are His bondslaves. The word "bondslave" speaks of one whose will is so swallowed up in the will of his Master that he has no regard for his own life.

When you have come to that place, you will be a weapon in the Master's hands, reaping such destruction in the enemy's camp that Satan will fear you as he did Paul. Thus, you will be one walking in the highest ranks of the overcomers.

The Bible says God will make you as a sword of a mighty man. (See Zechariah 9:13.) And the Spirit wields the sword. (See Ephesians 6:17 *Amplified.*) But He can only wield a sword over which He has complete control. The more control He has, the more powerful and destructive the sword will be against the enemy's rank and file.

To show you how crucial obedience is, I'd like to share a story with you. One night the Lord woke me up to pray. As I prayed, I saw a man who was flying a plane in the dark at low altitude. Search lights flashed above him. In the vision, I clearly saw the look of terror on his face. The Lord spoke and told me this man was running drugs and would die destined for hell if I wasn't faithful to pray. So I prayed for a few hours there in the darkness. I prayed until the burden was released.

A few weeks later, my friend Melinda and I went to a friend's home for dinner. When we walked in, the man I had seen in the vision was sitting in the kitchen. I didn't say anything until we all sat down to dinner, said grace, and began to eat.

As this man was taking a bite of his steak, I looked him straight in the eye and began to tell about what had taken place a few weeks before. My opening statement was: "If I had not prayed for you at such and such a time while you were foolishly running drugs in a plane, you would be dead right now."

Five hours later, he gave his life to Christ. Tears streamed down his face onto the opened Bible laying in front of him. Satan lost, and God won because someone was obedient to pray.

OBEDIENCE SAYS IT ALL

God needs intercessors who are obedient to the call to prayer. His eyes are continually open, searching the world for faithful warriors who delight in doing the Master's bidding. Time is of the essence when the Spirit calls. Consequently, prompt obedience must become a way of life.

A dear and special lady named Esther Marocco tells of the day God called her to urgent prayer. Waking her early, the Holy Spirit said: "You must pray like you use to in the mission field when danger was at hand. Pray now so you can comfort the others later." Esther prayed obediently, grievously pouring out her strength, only to be filled anew with the Lord's strength. It felt wonderfully and peacefully familiar. She wondered what was about to happen that would require such powerful intercession.

It wasn't long before the answer came. Esther's husband died of a heart attack. But she *was* strong, and her strength and comfort went out to her adult children. Each in turn and in his or her own way needed what Esther had acquired in prayer. God mercifully prepared and sustained their mother through the entire crisis. How different it might have been had she not been obedient to the Spirit's call.

I came to such a crisis in my own life and ministry. The Lord awoke me one morning to a vision of an impending peril, and I wept and prayed for over two hours. I felt in my heart that to be victorious under the coming attack I would have to fast and pray like never before. I would need explicit directions both for prayer and follow-through in the course of ministry.

After prayer, the Lord began to speak to me through His Word. For several days He called me at varying times of the day or in the middle of the night to travail against the destruction. Each time the prayer was followed by specific instructions from the Word.

By the end of the first few days, I knew I was facing my own Gethsemane experience. I asked myself, 'Would I be willing to bear such a cross to answer the call on my life?' Did the souls on the other side of this seemingly ominous battle count enough to go through what seemed like death's door? I knew that through much of the trial I would stand alone. Could I be obedient—even to the death that lay before me?

I had experienced Gethsemanes before. As painful as each cross had been, obedience to my Lord had released the grace to win each war. Did I love the Lord enough to follow Him through the hard times as well as the good?

But He Himself had told me: "When there are not enough words to say I love you, obedience says it all!"

Yes, I loved the Lord and all He stood for. Obedience would bring the grace to bear even this cross.

I began a season of fasting and prayer. With each session of prayer, God instructed me through His Word. At the end of about three months of fasting two meals a day, praying, and seeking Him in the Word, the enemy's plan was clear. My plan of action was equally as obvious. Of course, as the months rolled on more would be given. But I knew that if I continued in prayer, spent time in the Word, and just as importantly, was *obedient* both to His call to special times of intercession and His directions, I would prevail.

This battle raged like a terrible nightmare for about a year and a half. Sometimes I wondered if I would make it. But God's love kept calling me on, and I followed.

Looking back, I realize how important it was to be obedient to the months of fasting and prayer before the storm hit. I believe that it was God's preparation for me to reach the other side of that storm in absolute victory. Had I not been obedient, I'm not sure I would have made it.

Isaiah 65:24 says: *"Before they call, I will answer."*

Obedience is the hardest thing you will ever do—obedience to pray when praying gets rough or to walk the path you've been called to when victory seems impossible. But I've learned if you are not going to be obedient to the Lord, then there is no sense praying. Disobedience sets up roadblocks that prohibit answers to prayer from being released. Therefore obedience, in turn, makes a clear path for the Lord to meet us graciously at our need.

If love pulls the cart of obedience, then obedience is the cart that carries the answers to prayer.

Further, anyone who desires to live the life of the overcomer will learn that little is as important as obedience. As time moves forward and as a Christian you mature, you will find that God will extend to you various degrees of yokes of His kingdom's government. Each yoke will be significantly more demanding than the yoke before it. You have earned the privilege of those yokes through obedience, yet you will find that in each graduation greater obedience is required. Two cannot walk together except they are agreed. So, the Lord will bring you into increasing levels of obedience to Himself by molding your will and binding it to His own. As this delicate process continues ever increasing maturity results. Through it all God will bring you into the camp of the mighty where overcomes dwell.

Chapter 9 ————————————————

The Secret To Effective Prayer

Nearly a century old, Abraham had been walking with God in a peculiar separation unto Himself for about twenty-five years when one day the Lord appeared to him. God's opening remark was: *"I am the Almighty God [El Shaddai]; walk before me, and be thou perfect"* (Genesis 17: 1).

Two revelations were given to Abraham in this statement. First, God let him know with Whom he was dealing: El means "strong one" or "the transcendent, the omnipotent, the might, the power." *Shaddai* means "double-breasted One" or "the One who nourishes, supplies, and satisfies." God was telling Abraham that *only* He could nourish, supply, and bless him. The Lord is the all-sufficient, all-bountiful One.

The second revelation received in this statement was the requirement put on Abraham that would enable him to remain eternally in this new relationship with his Creator. He was to "walk before God and be perfect."

"Be perfect?" you ask. Impossible! How could God ask that of Abraham?

To begin with, God would never ask anyone to do anything He hadn't given him the grace to do. In His opening address to Abraham, God was saying *I am* the source that will enable you to be obedient to My command. It was then Abraham's responsibility to drink from the spring of life opened up to him, thus filling himself with power to obey.

In *The Amplified Bible*, we find a slightly different rendering of this verse that sheds more light on God's words: "I am the Almighty God; walk and live *habitually* before Me, and be perfect—blameless—whole-hearted, complete." (italics added.)

We see here that only the act of walking or living habitually before God (El-Shaddai) will enable a person to be perfected. The word "perfect" in Hebrew is *tamam*, which means "to come to the full" or "to reach that perfect state." In Greek it is *teleios*, from the two root words *telos*—to "set out for a *definite* goal" —and *olo*—to "bring forth." In New Testament writings, *teleios* means "to be perfected in the divine nature."

Romans 6:22 says: "Now being made free from sin, and become servants to God, ye have your fruit unto holiness, and the end everlasting life."

The word "holiness," *hosios*, is the divine nature. It means "sacred, pure, sure, and merciful." The word "sure" means to "foster as a parent," which was God's promise to Abraham: "I can and will foster your growth as a parent."

In the word "merciful," we see God's character as displayed toward man. Without His mercy we would all be doomed for hell. Because of His mercy, however—by the instrumentality of His grace, by and through Jesus Christ and His blood shed for us while we were yet sinners, hating the ways of God—we are saved if we have accepted His forgiveness.

Embodied, then, in the nature of God is a forgiving heart.

In short, God was telling Abraham to take on His own nature. Jesus said the same thing in His Sermon on the Mount:

> *You, therefore, must be perfect, as your heavenly Father is perfect [that is, grow into complete maturity of godliness in mind and character, having reached the proper*

height of virtue and integrity]—
Matthew 5:48 *Amplified.*

This is directed right at the Church. It is not a suggestion but a command. And—praise be to God—He has given us the power to fulfill His Word!

HOW IS YOUR HEART?

As children of God, we should want Him with every atom of our being. We want His healing, His victory, His love, and His provisions. But do we want His nature, His communion, or His burden? Do we want those who have offended us to be healed and to experience God and His love? Do we want the millions of souls who are perishing to be saved? Do we want battle-worn saints to be strengthened and revitalized in Christ? If not, *why not?*

Many of us have simply made the mistake of exchanging God's burden for Satan's burden. Right at the top of the list is *unforgiveness.* King David said: "O God, *you are my God, earnestly I seek you; my soul thirsts for you, my body longs for you, in a dry and weary land where there is no water*" (Psalm 63:1 *NIV*).

The Holy Spirit is the water that satisfies the soul and is received through prayer and spending time in the Word. As His water nurtures us, we are to yield our fruit of plenty to all who are in need. Why then, are our hearts often unable to absorb the water needed to yield a spiritual harvest?

I come from the San Joaquin Valley in California. One of the things this valley is known for is a type of soil called *hardpan.* It's so hard that you can't dig into it; instead, you have to dynamite through it. The soil is like cement, and since it doesn't absorb water well, rainwater often just lies on top of the ground until it evaporates. Consequently, farmers are extremely limited in what kind of crops they can grow. With the exception of evergreen and fig trees, this soil is useless for any kind of agriculture.

The heart of a sinner before regeneration is as hard as *hardpan*. But once the spirit is inhabited by the Holy Spirit, He immediately goes to work and slowly develops a soft, fleshy heart.

The San Joaquin Valley also contains a soil called *river bottom*. Rich in everything needed for the highest yields in farming, it is soft and can accommodate most of a rancher's needs. This depicts the heart of a saint yielded to the Holy Spirit. Walking in obedience to God's laws, his heart is being "perfected."

The key to turning a heart like *hardpan* into a heart like *river bottom* is easy to grasp. While expounding on the ways of love, Jesus clarified through His teaching that the ways of God are not the ways of man. Every word He speaks cuts right through the heart of self-righteousness and the facades with which people surround themselves.

Jesus said to love *(agape)* your enemies and do good to those who hate you. Then He even said to bless your abusers and to give without expecting anything in return. In other words. "*As you would like and desire that men would do to you, do exactly so to them*" (*Luke 6:31 Amplified*). Unless your life is dominated by Christ rather than self, it will be impossible for you to be obedient to these love commands.

GETTING WHAT YOU GIVE

In previous chapters we discussed love, humility, the fruits of the Spirit, and obedience. We dealt with these before approaching the subject of forgiveness because if the opposites of these graces rule your life, they will prohibit your ability to forgive. Hate, anger, pride, lust, self-centeredness, jealousy, and rebellion are all elements that make a heart as hard as *hardpan*. A heart this hard cannot bear the fruit of forgiveness. And without a forgiving heart, God won't forgive you.

Jesus further says that if you love those who love you, what credit is that to you? Anyone can do that. If you're kind to those who are kind to you and lend expecting to have your good deeds returned to you, how can you think that makes you good? You haven't proven love by these things. You're only fooling yourself. (See Luke 6:32-34.) Then the Lord repeats Himself. This lesson is so important that it has to be reinforced.

> But love *[agape]* *your enemies,*
> *and be kind and do good—doing*
> *favors so that someone derives ben-*
> *efits from them; and lend expecting*
> *and hoping for nothing in return,*
> *but considering nothing as lost and*
> *despairing of no one; and then your*
> *recompense (your reward) will be*
> **great—rich, strong, intense**
> **and abundant**—*and you will be*
> *sons of the Most High; for He is*
> *kind and charitable and good to the*
> *ungrateful and the selfish and*
> *wicked. So be merciful—sympa-*
> *thetic, tender, responsive and*
> *compassionate — even as your*
> *Father is [all these]—Luke 6:35,*
> *36 Amplified.* (emphasis author's)

After telling us what to do, Jesus shared the principles to live by that will enable us. Don't judge—you won't be judged. Don't condemn— you won't be condemned. Forgive—you'll be forgiven. (See verse 37.)

When someone hurts you, you judge their motives, their understanding of the situation, and their heart. Having judged them, you will automatically condemn them. The next logical step will be unforgiveness. You ask yourself: "Why should I forgive so and so after what they did to me? They were wrong."

If not dealt with, unforgiveness will become bitterness, which will beget unresolved anger and fear. Once this is played out, you will find yourself unable to love anyone and distrusting of everyone. You will be constantly judging, condemning, and criticizing everyone from your pastor to the gas station attendant. Your children, your mate, and your parents will become targets. Self-pity and loneliness will set in.

Once set in motion, all of God's laws have a recycling effect. Just as rain comes down, and through evaporation rises back up to the clouds, only to come down again, your own actions will set the wheels in motion that bring them back to you. As the Lord said,

> Give [judgments, condemnation, unforgiveness], and it will be given you. A good measure, pressed down, shaken together and running over, will be poured into your lap. For with the measure you use, it will be measured to you—Luke 6:38 NIV. (emphasis in brackets, authors.)

RELEASE YOUR BURDEN

When we sinned against the Lord through Adam, the increase of our knowledge intensified the greatness of our sin. Even so, God didn't judge us. He gave the Law so we could judge ourselves. Then He sent Christ to free us from condemnation. But He still didn't judge us.

Even at the Great Throne Judgment, it will be the Word of Truth that will judge man's wretchedness, not a judgmental, critical heart of unforgiveness laboring in the Lord.

God reaps a kingdom born in love as He continues to plant the seed of forgiveness (Christ Jesus) in the hardened hearts of repentant people.

Jesus gave us an important parable:

> *Can the blind lead the blind? shall they not both fall into the ditch? The disciple is not above his master: but every one that is perfect shall be as his master.... A good man out of the good treasure of his heart bringeth forth that which is good; and an evil man out of the evil treasure of his heart bringeth forth that which is evil: for out of the abundance of the heart his mouth speaketh*—Luke 6:39, 40, 45.

If a person is blinded by all the burdens of an unforgiving heart, he or she cannot lead another.

On the other hand, you can *decide* to learn to walk the ways of a higher order of love in Christ. By releasing the heavy burdens in your heart, you will be a well of life to others.

In the Mosaic law, the Jews were commanded to rest on the Sabbath and not defile it. By the time Jesus arrived, that law had evolved to the point where one could not carry so much as an earring or a nose ring on the Sabbath; for that was considered a burden and therefore, worthy of death.

Now we know that Christ is the true rest or Sabbath. Yet in Him we carry burdens much heavier than trying to lift an ox out of a hole with our bare hands, let alone an earring! Those burdens are bitterness, anger, fear, etc. All these burdens, however, stem from one seed called *unforgiveness*.

Root up your burdens, and they will be replaced with love, peace, and joy. We know that perfect love casts out all fear, (1 John 4:18), and avails us of an open communion with the Lord. When you let go of the burden, God will take it. *He will heal you and the situation.*

Only when you are free of the burden of unforgiveness can you stand beneath the open fountain of fresh living water, bathe your soul, and bring your anxieties to rest. You'll begin a cycle of harvesting good things, for love will bring answers to prayer. With your spiritual vision wonderfully clear, you'll see people and situations through God's eyes. This doesn't mean there will be no more problems, but you will handle them with the power of God.

OPENING THE DOOR TO RECONCILIATION

God forgave us, and forgiveness opens the door of reconciliation. Reconciliation means to restore friendship or communion.

If reconciliation is utterly impossible, then give that burden to the Lord and let Him heal you based on your willingness for reconciliation. Such an action will help you grow in maturity.

Just as an adolescent's goal is to grow up and become like his mother or father, our goal as Christians is to increase in Christlikeness. In turn, this will produce a richer yield of harvest from our prayers.

Jesus said of His Father: " I know that you always hear Me, for I always do the things that are pleasing to You" (John 11:42, 8:29, paraphrased).

While our faith is not based on works, works are necessarily an outgrowth of our faith. Even so, if we believe in Jesus Christ, we believe in His forgiveness. This allows us the privilege of open communication with Him. In turn, we must believe that we, too, must forgive others in their trespasses and sins against us if we are to continue in fellowship with Him. The same One who said: "Father, forgive them," also said that we must forgive. (Luke 23:34; see also Mark 11:25, 26).

Obedience to God's Word is a sure path to answered prayer. Our goal is to become as effective in prayer as possible. And a person is only as effective as his willingness to live a life of forgiveness.

When the cycle of forgiveness stops, you will eventually

become so hardened in bitterness that it will cause a shipwreck of your faith. Your spiritual life will crumble to ruin and, unfortunately, cause others around you to fall. (See Hebrews 12:15.) Consequently, there will be no harvest because there will no longer be any prayer. Although unforgiveness is fatal to the life of faith, forgiveness still can be the hardest thing you will ever do. However, if you want peace in your life, you must sow seeds of forgiveness.

CHOOSING TO FORGIVE

I have had the opportunity to put the law of forgiveness into action many times in my Christian walk. In the past it was at times relatively easy; other times it would take weeks to work out my anger and finally enter into the healing rest of forgiveness. (Admittedly today forgiveness has become so natural that the process is completed in my heart before injury can ever occur.)

The most difficult act of forgiveness I have ever experienced was to forgive my brother-in-law, who raped my 14 year old daughter. The *decision* to forgive came immediately for both Ricci and me, *but walking it out* until every root was gone was quite another story.

When I received the call telling me that my beautiful teenage daughter had been raped, I felt as though I were standing on the fault line of an earthquake. It had actually taken place two days before, but because of the shock and the intricacy of the people involved, it took Ricci that long to share what had happened.

I had been in prayer constantly the day of the violation, greatly concerned about Ricci, who was three thousand miles away. When I called to see if she was all right, she assured me she was fine, although she sounded distant. The following day, I prayed fervently again and then spent another restless night.

The next day, when the call came, I couldn't believe how calm I was on the outside—on the inside, I was shaking so badly I could hardly walk. I talked calmly with both my sister and her husband, then with Ricci. My mind was reeling. How could this man do such a thing to his own niece?

I had to get Ricci home safely, away from his reach. Yet my sister was falling apart at the seams in deeper shock than I was. She felt responsible, disillusioned that her whole world had come crashing down—and she was helpless to stop it. She cried deeply, heaving sobs because her pain was so unbearable.

My thoughts raced. How can I help her? Her own daughter is in as much agony as mine. What do I do about *him*—the man responsible for all this pain unleashed upon all the people whom I love so? I am so far away.... I couldn't make the spinning in my mind go away.

Mechanically, I called the airlines to get Ricci home, tried to calm my hysterical roommate, and prayed. Plans were made to get Ricci to the airport, and within fifteen minutes she was out of the house and on her way. My sister also left their home—to go where, I didn't know. She was in terrible shape, and I was frightened.

I talked to her husband and told him I forgave him. No, I wouldn't prosecute him because I wasn't sure my sister and niece—or Ricci, for that matter—could hold up under such a trial. We talked for almost half an hour. By the time we were done he had given his life to the Lord—I thought.

Once I found my sister, I called her every fifteen minutes or so until I knew she would make it through the initial shock. It was a three-and-a-half-hour drive to the airport, but it took me several extra hours because I kept stopping to call my sister. By the time Ricci stepped off the plane, I hoped that the worst was over.

That night I held my trembling child in my arms as she unveiled the whole wretched story, often stopping to fight off hysteria. It took a while, but I knew how crucial it was for her to open up completely in order to allow God to begin His long season of healing. Together, we cried and forgave this man again.

But Ricci had changed—fear ruled her. She wouldn't go from one room to another without someone with her. All the drapes had to stay shut. Endless nightmares haunted her sleep. What seemed like a hundred times a day, Ricci would walk into the bathroom and redo her make-up; she sought constant confirmation that she was pretty, loved, and protected. Again, I would have to forgive!

Suddenly, another dramatic change came—Ricci ran away from home! Again, I forgave the perpetrator.

Many calls to my family followed. After weeks, I finally began to hear life in my sister's voice. How many times would I have to *choose* to forgive while struggling to pick up the shattered pieces of my entire family?

Angry and wounded, Ricci was unreachable. Time seemed to be our worst enemy. She felt God had forsaken her, and I couldn't convince her otherwise. She no longer had a need for Him!

Over the next year many things occurred that finally led my sister to leave her husband. With each new discovery of the destruction he had caused—even to his own daughter—divorce soon proved to be the only option that would fully protect everyone involved. It took my sister over a year to come to a place of healing within herself where she could begin to forgive her ex-husband. Her daughter is still undergoing the healing of forgiveness.

As for Ricci, the Lord brought her to a place of divine healing and through a work of forgiveness in a single night! Shortly thereafter, she said it was the first time since the rape that she could hear "his" name without pain shooting through her heart. Now many years older, Ricci is once again the sweet girl who feels safe and secure with Jesus.

THE FRUIT OF FORGIVENESS

In forgiving my brother-in-law, I eventually led him to true repentance, dedication to the Lord, and the baptism of the Holy Spirit. I still pray for him and desire to see him answer the call that's on his life. But most of all I want the torment with which he has lived to be over. Only God can deliver from such torment, so it is God whom I seek on my brother-in-law's behalf.

Had I allowed a root of bitterness to poison me instead of seeking God until the decision I made with my mind became a healing stream flowing out of my heart, this story may have ended tragically. But because I could forgive, I was instrumental in helping each of my family members come into the healing of forgiveness. I prayed that they would answer God's call on their lives.

The Lord has done miracles through the obedience of forgiveness in the lives of the people I love. As the fruit of my prayers, they are *victories won in forgiveness*.

Perhaps someone has seriously offended you. They are in need of your forgiveness. If my sister's ex-husband had been lost because I couldn't forgive him, he would have been a soul lost to Jesus Christ. Nothing is worth that price!

When you forgive those who have offended you, you will become a new person. It may make a new person out of your offender, too. You will restore peace to your own heart and life.

David wrote:

> *Surely I have calmed and quieted my soul, like a weaned child with his mother; like a weaned child is my soul within me [ceased from fretting]*—Psalm 131:2 Amplified. *He makes me lie down in (fresh tender) green pastures; He leads me beside the still and restful waters*—Psalm 23:2 Amplified, italics added.
>
> *All my fountains are in you*—Psalm 87:7 NIV.

Do you feel that all is at rest? When you reach that mature and perfect nature Christ spoke about, you'll find the pastures fresh and tender. You will find silky grass under your feet, quiet streams, and water you can drink to your heart's delight. When you're at peace with God and man, all your fountains are clean and spring from the Lord.

The world around you may be in peril but you will be at rest, walking in the strength of God's peace and love, you will find the way to lead others from the troubled waters to peace, like your Master, Jesus. You will have a forgiving heart which indeed is a vital part of the bedrock of the heart of the overcomer. Through forgiveness, you overcome the world, the flesh and the devil. Through true forgiveness you walk in identification with our Divine Mediator. Thus, you come to reflect His wonderful nature to those who need it most.

PART III

Winning In Christ

We first spoke of praying with an attitude that refuses to give up. We talked about God's desire to answer your prayers and the understanding needed to fuel the vehicle of perseverance. We then moved into the hindrances to prayer.

I once asked the Lord to give me more faith. His answer to me was: "It isn't more faith you need, it's more knowledge." I realized that He was referring to Jesus' statement that we could move mountains with as little faith as a *"grain of mustard seed" (Matthew 17:20)*. Also, the Bible says to every man is given the measure of faith. (See Romans 12:3.) In other words, the Lord has already taken care of the area of faith. *Now it's up to us to get the understanding!*

We need to understand the strategy of the devil if we are to confront his efforts to keep us out of our prayer closets. The Lord said: *"My people are destroyed for lack of knowledge" (Hosea 4:6)*.

The next section is designed to help you gain more knowledge about the Lord and the actual arena of prayer for the purpose of encouraging your faith to prevail.

Chapter 10————————————

To Know Him Is To Trust Him

Now that we have crawled out of the murky pool of "self," let's boldly jump into the fathomless ocean of God. The Holy Spirit says: *"Arise my darling, my beautiful one, and come with me" (Song of Songs 2:10 NIV).*

This is the constant wooing of the Holy Spirit to each of His own. "Arise, My darling," He sings to a sleeping bride. He is not calling to the body—it is strong and active—nor to the spirit—the Spirit of God dwells there. God's Holy Spirit speaks to our souls, which afore time were asleep. Dazed and lethargic, our senses numb with the drunkenness of sour wine.

We hear the Holy Spirit's cry, but it seems faint. Yet He sings: "Arise from the snares that bind you, My beautiful one." As He speaks, our hearts begin to yearn for fresh new wine. We see glimpses of love on the horizon, and our souls are stirred by the sound of His voice. Our love has been awakened!

Without His call we cannot come, for it's the Holy Spirit who carries us to the chambers of our Beloved. Do we dare remain sleeping when He calls? On the contrary, we rise and follow.

INTO HIS CHAMBERS

Prayer is born of the Spirit and must be developed and led by Him. He is the Master, and we must remain but putty in His lofty hands. We can fret and stew, tearing away at the doors that seem to separate us, but we will only weary ourselves and woefully slip away.

If we follow the Lord, however, we will see that He has already made the way. A small, winding path in the wilderness leads to His enchanting chambers where all the names of God, deep with meaning and power, are etched. Each new chamber holds a new experience within—a new name, a new love, a new joy. Consider a few of God's many names.

Friend of Sinners—What a friend is He who laid down His life for you and for me.

Rabbi—The teacher who imparts the wisdom of the ages will teach you His Word and His ways. He will make you wiser than your enemies and elevate you to a place of wisdom against which no one can stand.

The Shepherd—He who feeds and nurtures His precious sheep. Why walk aimlessly, groping in hopelessness? Jesus knows all your needs. Even your desires lay upon His tender heart. When you are nestled close to Him, you experience His tenderness. His rod is to guide and protect you, not to rule you in fear.

The Resting Place—Are you weary and faint from the struggles of life? Come abide in Christ. When the world weighs too heavily on your heart, demanding too much in too little time, Jesus Christ will give you rest.

My Glory—Leaving all that is dull we seek the resplendent glow of the One who alone is our glory. Without Him we are naked and ashamed. With Him, we are clothed in glory.

Light of the Morning—When night has assailed us with its terrors and woes, we are led into the chamber of His glorious light, and our fears seem to melt as we bask in its warmth.

Author and Finisher of our Faith—No battles here; we rest, and He does the work when our hearts are screaming: "It can't be done!" As the world around us raises its voice in harmony with the impossible, we are called to come and bathe in the pools of our Creator, who will complete in us the good work He has begun.

The Living Bread—Are you hungry today? Come partake of Him who will satisfy as no one else can. We hunger—for what, we don't know. Our spirits cry out for the heavenly manna—our flesh for the things of the world. When we are done yet still unfed, we can at last come and receive from the Lord life-giving bread. Day by day the taste gets sweeter until even our flesh is satisfied with Him and Him alone.

King of Israel—Grow in adoration, and dance before your King. When you're in His company, who can stand before you? Princes fall before Him and kingdoms are ruled by Him. When He is your King, He is your safety.

The Balm of Gilead—Is your heart in need of healing? Is your soul reeling from the attacks of the evil one? As the Balm flows down over your heart, wounds are mended with cool, refreshing salve that heals all.

My Beloved—Do you need to be loved? Do you feel alone or forsaken? Sing your song to your Beloved and find the heights of His love. None can love like Him, for only He is willing to pour His oceans of love upon an empty vessel with hands uplifted and ready to drink. Although the world turns away from you, He never will.

Hiding Place—Who can find you when He is your hiding place? You can crawl deep inside Him, shut off the painful world outside, and rest. He will protect and provide for you. The Lord will make a way while you are reposed in His hand.

A Diadem of Beauty—Out of Zion, the perfection of beauty shines forth. Stay with Him, hide in Him, and lie before Him. Like Moses when he came down from the mountain, He will become your diadem of beauty, and His radiance will shine from your face.

Pearl of Great Price—When you turn away from all the entanglements of the world to the heavenly prize, open your hand and find the Pearl of Great Price. Who can adore you more or ever give you more? Who is as beautiful, perfect, or altogether lovely as He?

Follow the Holy Spirit, He will carefully lead you into each new chamber. He may hide you away in one chamber for weeks or months before you see another. In His infinite wisdom He will always do what is best. Speak to Him and ask: "Holy Spirit, please lead me in to know Jesus." That is why He came—to teach of Jesus.

RUNNING WITH THE KING

The Spirit has called, and you answered. Now as the Holy Spirit leads you into the royal chambers, the King enters to meet with you.

When the Holy Spirit touches your heart, go with Him quickly. Don't hold back. Excuse yourself from whatever else calls and run with Him. Here in the solitude of the moment will come the expressions for which you've waited. You'll never know heaven's bliss amid the noise and clatter of the world's demands. Don't be confused; you can run with Jesus while resting at His feet.

Make your petitions known. Ask the gentle Spirit of God: "Teach me to rest when the cloud rests and to flow when it moves." Tell Him your heart's desire. He is a ready listener. The Holy Spirit moves slowly and gently, so get in touch with His speed. Calm your spirit, and quietly rest at His feet. The psalmist wrote: *"I wait for the Lord, my soul waits"* and *"Find rest, O my soul, in God alone"* (Psalms 130:5; 62:5 NIV). He leads, and we follow. We call out to Him: "Take me away with You; please hurry!"

When Martha complained that Mary wasn't helping with the chores, Jesus quieted Martha. Mary's heart was running with Jesus, and He wouldn't deny her that—for it was He who had called. If only Martha had heard the call, too.

The psalmist cried: *"As the hart pants and longs for the water brooks, so I pant and long for You, O God* (Psalm 42:1 Amplified).

As he cried these words, David could see in his mind a deer running through a wilderness thicket to find the shaded watering place that would provide refuge. As its pursuer ran even harder, the hart would dart frantically, longing for the drink that would refresh and the shelter that would hide his scent. How he desired the cool, revitalizing plunge that would give new strength to his tired body! Like David, you must crave the Lord with your whole mind, body, and soul and run to Him like a hart after water. Then you can rest your weary mind and body at His feet.

"Listen! My lover! Look! Here he comes, leaping across the mountains, bounding over the hills" (Song of Songs 2:8 NIV).

"Leaping across the mountains" speaks of the resurrection life in which Christ comes to you. Putting all things beneath His feet—with every obstruction moved out of the way—He comes quickly and joyously to melt His heart with yours and show you His abounding grace. He has given you His power and authority and has called you from the valley to reign with Him on Mount Zion. Nothing can separate Him from you.

You see Him now in ways you never have before. With your innermost being enthroned in His will He has become the only source of life from which you draw. Now you know Him in His resurrection. Although trials are all around you, your heart has learned to be at rest in His ever-present and tender care.

LIFE ON THE ROCK

Once you have learned to share the Lord's heart and knowledge and feel confident in His power, you will enter into an exciting period of battle against the enemy for needs in your own life and the lives of others. With this new understanding and freedom in your life, God calls you to see the world through His eyes, which see victory in all things through Jesus Christ.

"Look from the top of Amana, from the top of Shenir and Hermon, from the lions' dens, from the mountains of the leopards" (Song of Songs 4:8). The Holy Spirit has called you to look from Amana, which means "confirmation of truth." You look at life through the eyes of truth. Confirmed in Christ, you can rest steadfastly on the Rock that cannot give way.*

*Ask for authors book "Canticles of The Exchanged Life" an exposition on song of Solomon.

"If any man is in Christ, he is a new creature; the old things passed away; behold new things have come" (2 Corinthians 5:17 NASB).

Walking the new life through Christ, you're not looking *for* the mountain of truth but *from* the mountain of truth. You are like the Word upon which you stand—a mountain or a mighty fortress, you have been tried and proved. The Word is confirmed in your life, and you run in the strength of the Most High, drawing from His power that rests in the truth to which you have now become undeniably united.

The Holy Spirit beckons you to gaze from the top of *Shenir*, which means "flexible armor." His armor is flexible not rigid. His yoke is easy and His burden light. God does not rule in fear, but in love. His armor is designed to meet your needs—to shield and defend—not burden or tax. Do you know how to use your armor against Satan? If you have received your training well, you're properly covered in His wisdom and grace.

You are like one who *"rules over men righteously, ruling in the fear of God. [You] dawn on them like the morning light, when the sun rises on a cloudless morning, when the tender grass springs out of the earth, through clear shining after rain"* (2 Samuel 23:3,4 Amplified).

You wisely wage war against Satan, while you love God and submit to His authority. Your gracious and humble manner has made you great and respected among man. His favor is your shield.

SITTING IN THE SHADE

You are now one who has experientially died with Christ at the cross and have been raised with Him to new life! You are one with Him, *energized* by Him, *animated* by Him, *saturated* with Him, and *endowed* with His gifts and graces.

He has lifted you up to look from the peak of *Hermon*, which means "destruction of the enemy." You're not sitting beneath the cross, penitent and seeking God's gracious favor and victory.

You delightedly witness the destruction of the enemy time and time again. Like the apostle Paul, you "glory" only in the cross of Jesus Christ. (See Galatians 6:14.) Like Daniel, you have spent your nights in the lions' den and lived to give glory and honor to the King. It has become your *"delight to sit in his shade,"* and His fruit is sweet to your taste. He has taken you to the banquet hall, and His banner over you is love! (See Song of Songs 2:3,4.)

The Lord has become your continual feast. You dine at His table and relish in His love. All your fountains are in Him. (See Psalm 87:7.)

But growing has taken time. Understanding the things of God ripens with age. Entering into that delightful rest the first time is like standing at home plate and hitting your first home run. You stand in amazement as you watch it fly through the air. Like riding bareback on a galloping stallion, you feel a thrill race through your soul—you feel the wind in your face and excitement in your bones. It feels like you're one with the horse and one with the wind. It's a freedom that's rare, never to be forgotten.

Notice I have not once said you enter that rest through your own works. You can't ride the wind on a pogo stick. It's here that you find new strength to run the long race. But like a fine-tuned athlete, you have worked long and hard with the Holy Spirit to enter into this place.

By now you are seeing many great victories in your life. But it's here in the place of rest that, like other great men and women of prayer, you'll begin to see new releases of the dynamics of prayer. George Muller, who built orphanages and fed and raised thousands of children; Reese Howells who built a seminary and a children's home; and John Hyde, who brought revival into India—they all obtained victory through prayer. These men ran the greatest miles of their race once they entered into "the rest."

George Muller was asked: "Don't you get excited when the Lord brings in funds exactly as you prayed He would?"

"Of course not!" George replied.

Perplexed, the inquirer asked: "Why?"

Mr. Muller firmly replied: "If I didn't expect Him to answer, I wouldn't have asked." He continued "My reaction would come if He *didn't* answer."

That didn't mean that George Muller would only have to ask once for his petition. In fact, if the funds were late in coming, he would increase his prayer time until the answer came. At times he would set his orphans down at the table when the cupboards were bare. Muller had prayed earnestly for food before the supply ran out. But as they gave thanks, the food would be brought by some generous soul—just enough for the meal. At other times, they had plenty. It wasn't how much or how long he would have to pray; it was the attitude with which he prayed. George Muller knew that God would provide. In this new place of rest, you like Mr. Muller walk in the confidence that only God inspires in the heart.

MEETING EVERY CRISIS

I can remember the first time the Lord authorized a raise for this ministry. Until that time, I had always labored long and hard in prayer to see the funds come in. One day in June, we were ministering in Spokane, Washington. The Lord told me that day in prayer to figure out the expenses of the ministry and let Him know what we would need monthly—He would bring it in. Doing as I was told, the next day I presented to the Lord the figure at which I had arrived. He simply replied: "It's done." And it was. That exact amount started coming in every month.

Less than a year later, the car blew up on the way to the Midwest. We were only three hours outside of our hometown, Fresno, California and were expected in Omaha in less than a week.

Our needs were being met, but we didn't have any extra money to buy another car. So Melinda and I looked at each other, got out of the car, and started pushing. Suddenly I was struck down too ill to do anything but stay in bed. There we were in Sacramento with a broken car, broken minister, and little money. The attack had left me sick and weak. But I had peace.

I told Melinda that I felt a tremendous peace and that God was going to give us a miracle. Next I reminded her that the Lord had said just the day before that it was time for another car. So I called a man who owned a car dealership a few states away to see if we could buy a car from him and set up a payment schedule. Within two hours he called back and said: "I'm going to *give* you a car. I'll have a man drive it down to you; he'll be there in two days."

The timing for this miracle couldn't have been more perfect. It gave me time to rest before we had to be on our way. The day we left Sacramento, the Lord told me I would be healed by the first meeting in Omaha. I was!

As you enter into God's rest, you can meet every crises in peace, knowing that God won't let you down. The more you get to know Him, the more you'll trust Him and run to obey Him in things you may not even understand.

A couple of years ago we needed a thousand dollars within twenty-four hours for airline tickets. So I prayed, and I knew we would have it. A little while later I received a call from another ministry. They wanted to contribute one thousand dollars if we would stop by to pick it up. We were happy to comply with their request!

After we left their headquarters, the Lord told me to take the money and give it to *another* ministry. By this time it was nearly midnight, but I knew we had to obey. Arriving at the home of the head of the other ministry, we found him and his wife up praying. They needed one thousand dollars by midnight to cover an emergency.

That was great, but *we* still needed a thousand dollars by the next day. Melinda called the airline by chance and found that prices had gone down substantially overnight. In addition we now had an extra day to purchase our tickets. The money came in right on time. We bought the tickets and had money left over!

The Holy Spirit moves you into *His* rest as you're faithful in prayer. You simply begin to break the worry habit, and your energy then goes to the positive realm of faith. Why? Because you know Him! In knowing the Lord you have learned to trust Him, and in trusting Him you *love* Him all the more. That alone is what makes an ordinary man into a giant man of God.

You have been methodically raised to walk in the overcoming life with Christ. The fruits of the Spirit are lush and ripe and you are now walking in the 100 fold return that Jesus promised to those who love and obey Him. Satan is manifestly under your feet and you have been positioned by Jesus to walk with the kings of the kingdom. All this and more because you have become a person of prayer.

Chapter 11 ——————————————————

Petitioning The King

In the mid-eighties I was teaching at a Bible school. About 3:00 a.m. the Lord woke me up with a magnificent vision. As I beheld a person dressed in the priestly robe worn only by the high priest of the old covenant, the Holy Spirit quickened scriptures to me about each part of the garment, giving me an understanding of the prophetic value of the robe and its meaning to today's saint.

This garment sparkled and shimmered like a prism of light. Just before the vision ended the Lord said: "Nita, this is what My children are dressed in as they come before Me in intercession. Tell My children everywhere how beautiful they are to Me when they pray."

The next day I had a similar vision. The robe was the same, but the man wearing it looked like he was African. The more he prayed, the brighter the garment became, until all the darkness around him had turned to light.

I asked the Lord what He was telling me. He said: "He is one of My top intercessors. Great and precious treasures are born into the Kingdom through his prayers. Because he is faithful, I shall increase him even more. Tell him when you see him."

That night I scanned the large auditorium, hoping this man might attend the Bible school. Sure enough, there he was. I called him to the front. Surprisingly small in stature and quiet in nature,

I marveled as he approached the platform. I shared the word the Lord had given me for him, and he wept.

After the service that night, I asked about him, and the president of the school told me that he travels all over Africa. He goes in where the gospel has never been preached, makes himself a little shelter, and prays—he prays for days, weeks, or however long it takes until hindrances are pulled down. The missionaries then follow him in and reap a great harvest of souls. Then a church is established.

When we come before God in prayer, He sees us dressed in the same priestly robes as our Master, Jesus. For it is the Holy Spirit's ministry to nurture and transform us. The Bible says:

> *[That we might develop] until we all attain oneness in the faith and in the comprehension of the full and accurate knowledge of the Son of God; that [we might arrive] at really mature manhood—the completeness of personality which is nothing less than the standard height of Christ's own perfection—the measure of the stature of the fullness of the Christ, and the completeness found in Him*—Ephesians 4:13 Amplified, italics added.

In other words, God is bringing the Church into the maturity of Christ, endowing us with His nature, His character, and His power.

GLORY DISPENSERS

Christ is a King, a Priest, a Prophet and an Apostle. And that ministry is now infused in the Church—His Body—both individually and collectively.

God's Word says of the Church:

> You have made them a kingdom
> [royal race] and priests to our God,
> and they shall reign [as kings] over
> the earth!—Revelation 5:10
> Amplified.

For the testimony of Jesus is the spirit of prophecy—Revelation
19:10 .

Moses said:

> Would that all the Lord's people
> were prophets, and that the Lord
> would put His Spirit upon them—
> Numbers 11:29 Amplified.

Also, we know that Jesus is "a priest for ever after the order of
Melchizedek" (Psalm 110:4), and that:

> He has put all things under His feet
> and has appointed Him the univer-
> sal and supreme Head of the church
> (a headship exercised throughout
> the church), which is His body, the
> fullness of Him Who fills all in
> all—for in that body lives the full
> measure of Him Who makes every-
> thing complete—Ephesians 1:22,
> 23 Amplified, italics added.

Melchizedek was a king, priest, and prophet. Now we too, are
members of this new priestly order, of which Christ is the head.

Finally:

> Wherefore, holy brethren, partak-
> ers of he heavenly calling, consider
> the Apostle and High Priest of our

profession, Christ Jesus.—Heb. 3:1

This isn't to say that we are all prophets like the apostle Paul or Elijah. Neither are we all prophets of the four-fold ministry—apostles, *prophets*, evangelists, and pastor-teachers. (See Ephesians 4:11.)

We are *the prophetic company* of the Melchizedek order. This gives us the anointing we need to defeat Satan. The *kingship* gives us the authority we need to rule. The priestly office gives the body the honor of ministering to the Lord and administering the new covenant. Putting it all together, we have the authority, power, and duty of administration of the new covenant. The apostolic anointing gives the church the efficacious ministry of Jesus Himself. (This is soon to be released.) In short, we are to be glory dispensers! It is not our age, strength, or intelligence that enables us. We are able to minister because of our position in Christ.

I ministered in a church on the east coast about thirteen years ago. As the saints began to worship the Lord, I could sense that something unusual was about to happen. Looking around I saw children, one by one, leaving their seats and moving to the front of the church. Before long, it seemed that all the children were up front beautifully dancing in the spirit before the Lord.

It was obvious that these young ones were in touch with Jesus Christ. It looked so lovely I began to weep. Shortly, a word of prophecy was given, then tongues and interpretation, and then another prophecy—all through the children! The last word commanded that they go and lay hands on the sick. Each one of them began to go out into the audience and gently lay hands on people. When worship had ended, testimonies were given about the many healings that had taken place.

I asked the pastor how long this had been going on, and he said: "A couple of weeks. It's quite a phenomenon. We don't want to quench what the Holy Spirit is doing, so we' re waiting and watching."

These incredible children were acting as God's little "glory dispensers."

THE PRIESTLY ANOINTING

It is the office of priest that gives us the special right to enter God's presence by the blood of Christ. If we are to rule effectually as kings, we must first understand and perform the priestly ministry. And if we are ever to become the nation of prophets to the world, as God has ordained, we must first fulfill the office of priest.

Exodus 28:1 says: "*From among the Israelites take your brother Aaron and his sons with him, that he may minister to Me in the priest's office*" (Amplified).

By this we learn that we are set aside to minister to the Lord. This occurs during worship, communion, intercession, and as we minister to individuals.

When Mother Theresa was asked how she could handle living in India with the sick and dying, she replied: "I see each one as Jesus. As I bathe them and care for them, I picture the face of Jesus on each and every one. I love them as though each one was Jesus, put under my care."

God wants this same heart in each of His children. As a priest, our ministry is unto the Lord.

The garments of the high priest are **"*sacred* garments [appointed official dress set apart for special holy services] for honor and for beauty"** (Exodus 28:2 Amplified). (*The King James Version* says **"for glory and for beauty."**)

As you enter the prayer closet, you are adorned in a *sacred garment*. Each intricate part of this garment speaks of Christ. Adorned in Christ, you are sacred, holy, and set apart for good works.

It is a garment of *beauty*. The Word says: "*From Zion, perfect in beauty, God shines forth*" (Psalm 50:2 NIV.) We are Zion, and in Christ we are perfect in beauty. God shines through us.

It is a garment of *glory or light*. The Bible says, God makes His messengers "flames of fire." (See Psalm 104:4 *NIV*.) Overcomers will, like them, be dressed in "white" (translated *light*). We are dressed in the glory of the Lord, which is none other than the Holy Spirit.

Picture a saint standing before the Lord and praying, perhaps quietly in his own prayer language. No one can hear him but the Lord. If you could see into the spiritual realm however, instead of a person you would see a glow growing brighter and brighter until all you saw was a huge flame of fire. We are encased in a garment of glory!

It is a garment of *honor*. Honor means power with God. The Bible tells us we are "crowned" with "glory and honor." (See Psalm 8:5.) We are spiritual Israel, which means "prince." When we stand before the throne of God, through and in Christ, we stand in a position of honor and have heaven's attention. More importantly, we have the Lord's individual attention.

STANDING YOUR GROUND

One of Satan's greatest tools is *deception*. He wants you convinced that your prayers are powerless against him. He'll do anything he can to keep your eyes off the Lord and on the problem that he has created.

If he is successful, you'll soon become so discouraged you won't even try to use the power that's within you to defeat him. You'll forget that you have a place of honor before God in Christ—an honor that Satan does *not* have. Consequently, the devil will be able to come in and steal your heart's desire away. To him, it's like taking candy away from a baby.

Note that I said *steal*; since Satan has no honor before God, he has no right to your belongings. If he is able to take them, it's because somewhere, sometime, you forgot *Whose* you were and who the devil is. You lost your perspective.

When I was ministering in Texas, I was introduced to the church's most effectual prayer warrior. During my stay, I spent some time talking with Sharon. During one of our conversations she shared an interesting story with me.

When she was first saved, Sharon was tremendously frightened by even the thought of Satan's presence. One day in prayer, the Lord gave her a vision. She said it was like standing in front of a movie screen. She saw Satan grasping her child in a stranglehold. Without thinking, she commanded him in the name of Jesus to release the boy and to be gone. Immediately, the devil vanished, and her son was all alone. Then Jesus appeared and spoke tenderly to her, saying: "It's just like that; you don't have to be afraid. He is under your foot in My name. Even so, he will not have your son. So be of good comfort."

You have honor with God, and you're wearing a garment of power. Satan is loathed by God, and he has no legal power.

Several years ago, I had a burden for a pastor of a church in Canada. God had moved mightily in the midst of his work, and the church was exploding in growth.

But then a satanic attack came with both barrels wide open. As the Lord gave me the burden, I felt impressed to begin praying and fasting. I called the pastor and shared my concern, along with my spiritual involvement on their behalf.

As the storm raged, many lies were spread that eventually brought the church board together to vote about whether or not to let the pastor go. During my prayer, I felt strongly impressed that he wasn't to be concerned; God would defend him and Satan would lose an important battle. I left that message with his secretary.

A couple of months later, I called the pastor, and he said the meeting that was held to vote him out ended up being the turning point of the Lord's victory. Not only did the vote turn out in his favor, but the men repented for not standing behind him. Consequently, a greater unity than ever before developed in the church and turned the tide of events. They saw great glory as the Lord generously intervened.

Satan lost that battle because some intercessors believed for God's best, fought the battle, and gained the victory.

THE INTERCESSOR'S HEART

The colors of the priestly garment are also significant. God commanded Moses to gather gold, blue, purple, scarlet, and fine (white) linen. (See Exodus 28:5.) *Gold* stands for His deity—the power of our authority; *blue*, His throne in heaven—the position of our rule; *purple*, His royalty—the headship of our rule; *scarlet*, His blood, that bought our right to rule; *white*, His righteousness—our covering and eternal destiny to rule.

Each part of the priestly garment symbolizes the salvation story and our ministry in Christ as an intercessor.

Over the garment, the Lord commanded them to: *"make the ephod of gold, of blue, and of purple, of scarlet, and fine twined linen, with cunning needle work"* (Exodus 28:6).

The *ephod*, an elegant jacket-like garment that fit over the robe, was held together by two shoulder pieces. The breastplate of judgment, the *Urim* and *Thummim*, and the precious jewels were all permanently attached to the ephod. Distinctive only of the high priest, he carried on it the weight of Israel. This lovely garment spoke of the zeal of God for His own.

Speaking of Christ, the Bible says He "was clad with zeal [and furious divine jealousy] as a cloak" (Isaiah 59:17 *Amplified*).

How pleasing you are to Him as you array yourself in this same divine zeal for the cares of God's heart.

All of this was bound together with the *"curious girdle"* of the ephod. (*Exodus 28:8.*) This was a long belt. Wrapping around the waistline of the high priest about three times, it fit over the ephod and hung down nearly to the floor. This belt spoke of the Spirit of intercession. Paul called it the *"belt of truth,"* (Ephesians 6:14), that penetrated so deep into the soul that it engulfed the *"bowels of mercies,"* (Colossians 3:12), and would eventually draw the believer to the cross of intercession.

Wrapped in pouches of gold that dangled from the high priest's shoulder on gold chains were two stones that carried the names of the twelve tribes of Israel. He wore them into the holy of holies as a memorial to the Lord:

> *And thou shalt take two onyx
> stones, and grave on them the
> names of the children of Israel: six
> of their names on one stone, and
> the other six names of the rest on
> the other stone, according to their
> birth*—Exodus 28:9, 10.

The pouches of gold in which the onyx stones were wrapped speak of the purity of the intercessor's heart. Christ's heart was spun in the pure gold of love; ours must be also. James warns us not to pray selfishly but rather to draw close to God, feel His heart, and then pray. (See James 4: 3 .)

These stones speak of the cross Christ carried on His shoulder and of the cross that we are to carry. Jesus said: *"If any man will come after me, let him deny himself, and take up his cross, and follow me"* (Matthew 16:24).

The cross of intercession is a cross of denial. There may be times you will want to have lunch with a friend, but the Holy Spirit will move on you in a spirit of intercession. Lunch will have to be cancelled or postponed *when the Lord has need of you.*

An Oregon pastor tells of a time when he was in need of prayer. While on a missionary journey, he was traveling along a winding, treacherous mountain road filled with potholes and craters. Unfortunately, he didn't know until it was too late that the road had been condemned by the government.

As he drove, clumps of the road gave way under his car and fell down the hillside. Yet he safely arrived at his destination—his car apparently carried by an invisible hand.

What he didn't know was that the invisible hand was the hand of *prayer!* As he drove up and down the dreadful road, one of God's faithful vessels of prayer stayed on her knees interceding on her pastor's behalf until he was out of danger. What did it cost her? Lost hours of sleep. The prize however, was worth the price!

SEEING THROUGH GOD'S EYES

The breastplate of judgment, (Exodus 28:15), carried twelve precious stones upon it—one valuable stone for each Hebrew tribe. Worn over the heart, it was permanently attached to the ephod by chains of gold.

The book of Hebrews teaches us that Christ came to fulfill or complete the purpose of Aaronic priesthood. He went into the heavenly holy of holies under the Aaronic priesthood, wearing the breastplate of judgment. He came out wearing the breastplate of righteousness under the Melchizedek priesthood. (See Isaiah 59:17.) Consequently, we too, have put on the breastplate of righteousness. (See Ephesians 6:14.)

This spiritual garment covers our heart. By it we know we are cleansed by Christ's blood. We now stand with this breastplate arrayed in precious stones, which act as a memorial before the Lord.

Speaking of Israel, of which we are a part, the Word says: "*For they shall be as the [precious] jewels of a crown, lifted high over and shining glitteringly upon His land*" (Zechariah 9:16 Amplified).

God sees His children as precious jewels that would look handsome on any king's crown. That's how we must see people, speaking words of perfection and truth over them. We carry the gems of God's children upon our golden heart of intercession.

I'll never forget a story that a pastor's wife shared with me one Sunday evening. In tears, she told me about their two sons. One was everything you could ever want a son to be. He always did and said the right things, never gave his parents any trouble, and entered the ministry to follow the Lord's calling on his life. He got married and became a great husband and father.

The other son was their oldest. He was quite a different story. While still in his late teens, he got involved with drinking, drugs, and girls. Sinking deeper and deeper into sin, he always embarrassed his parents and chased after things that would destroy him.

One night his parents kicked him out of the house, telling him that as long as he wouldn't live for God he couldn't live there.

Under the influence of drugs at the time, the young man ran out of the house, squealed his car out of the driveway, and raced off. With that, his mother went into her bedroom to fast and pray for two days. She cried, complained, ranted, and raved, bewailing the grief that her riotous son was causing. In the evening of the second day, the Lord spoke.

It was obvious that He was angry. "How dare you call yourself after My name?" God started. "I gave you a son to raise and to love. Do you think I didn't know he would go through these hard times when I gave him to you? Satan is rolling over him like a steamroller—and now you are adding insult to injury. *He* is the victim here. I want him to see My mercy and grace, yet you are only showing him wrath. Will you heal him or continue to cripple him because of your wounded pride?"

After that word, she ran out of the bedroom, called to her husband, and told him they had to find their son and stop Satan from destroying him. While driving to their son's hangouts, she explained what the Lord had said to her.

At about 2:00 a.m. the pastor and his wife finally found their son and asked him to come home. They told him how sorry they were and begged his forgiveness. They wept together, took him home, and decided to show him unconditional love. That was the turning point for him. Slowly, but surely, the fruits of their love and prayers emerged in their son. As they began to see him as a precious jewel that Satan was trying to steal and let their love become a protective shield around him, the young man began to feel important to God. That knowledge changed his destiny.

If our hearts are truly touching God's heart in prayer, then our actions and attitudes outside of the prayer closet will reflect it. As we see people through God's eyes, we will want to treat them the way Jesus would if He were dealing with them directly. Furthermore, our ability to do this reflects our growing Christian maturity. A maturity that we have attained through prayer.

READY AND ABLE

Kept inside a pocket on the priest's breastplate were two stones called the Urim and Thummim: "And thou shalt put in the breastplate of judgment the Urim and the Thummim; and they shall be upon Aaron's heart." (Exodus 28:30).

The word Urim literally means "lights." The word Thummim literally means "perfection," or "complete truth." Together they stand for the "light of complete or perfect truth." Up until the time of Solomon's reign these stones were used by the high priest to receive answers and direction from God. During the reign of David, however, the Lord began to speak to His people through His prophets more than by this previous method.

Today God communicates to believers through His Son by speaking to us in our spirit and by the Word. The two will always agree and bring peace.

Like the high priest, our garment would not be complete without the Word of God on our heart and an ear ready to listen should He decide to speak. You wouldn't want to miss any treasures the Lord might want to send your way.

The high priest also wore a long, blue robe called the robe of the ephod. (See Exodus 28:31.) Long enough to touch the ground, this robe was worn under the ephod. It had no seam, only a hole at the top for the priest's head. Along the hem were gold bells and pomegranates, alternating all the way around the hem:

> And it shall be upon Aaron to minister: and his sound shall be heard when he goeth in unto the holy place before the Lord, and when he cometh out, that he die not—
> Exodus 28:35.

The pomegranates symbolize the fruits of righteousness you bear through prayer, and the bells represent music. When a saint goes before the Lord in intercession, adorned in his priestly garment, he is music to the Lord's ears. His prayers are like a symphony that rises to the Father.

On his head the high priest wore a turban or holy crown. Attached to it was a golden plate with the words "holiness to the Lord" engraved on it. The priest wore it so he would bear the iniquity of the things offered to the Lord. *"And it shall be always upon his forehead, that they may be accepted before the Lord."* (Exodus 28:38).

Christ wore a "helmet of salvation upon his head" so we could wear the helmet of salvation, have the mind of Christ, and be cleansed of all unrighteousness. (See Isaiah 59:17; Ephesians 6:17, and 1 Corinthians 2:16.)

The Lord has chosen to work through vessels of clay. Apart from Christ, we are imperfect. Most of what we do for the Lord is imperfect. Of course the Lord's part is always perfect; it's our part, our motives, that need God's mercy.

THE HAPPY EXCHANGE

In 1994 The Lord visited me to talk with me about a few different things. While we were discussing the issues of our visit, I noticed something strange happening. About every 3 to 5 minutes, I would experience a murky transparent film leave my body like someone lifting off a cloak or a blanket and float through the air to fall gently upon Jesus. Each time this would occur, Jesus would smile. Then a clear transparent and radiant film would leave His hands, take the shape of a blanket, float through the air and gently fall upon me. Finally, I asked Him what was happening, and why He smiled each time this occurred.

He responded: Nita, your sin is ever being imputed to Me and My righteousness to you. That continues as long as you are on earth and until your sin nature is crucified and you have entered into union with Me. At that time My righteousness is imparted to you, and I live My life out through you. (II Corinthians 5:17-21). It is for our imperfection in God's work that we are covered by the crown that says: "holiness to the Lord."

Finally, the high priest wore an embroidered coat of fine linen. (See Exodus 28:39.) This coat was a pure white, full-length undergarment that fit under the robe. It represents "the righteousness of Christ." Once, I believe it was in 1993 while in prayer, I saw descending from heaven to rest upon me the radiant and lovely garment of righteousness. It was so beautiful and majestic all I could do was weep. This illustrious garment is ours by faith until we are amply perfected in Christ, at which time it is imparted. It remains the inner glow of purging fire that cleans and purifies everything it touches. It's the garment that no one but the Lord can see—and it tells Him we are His.

As our prayers go forth, energized by this holy fire, they destroy the works of Satan. This righteousness is an ensign, a holy standard against the enemy's interference. It's the glow that blinds the devil and blesses the Lord! This magnificent array of holy apparel wreaks destruction to all that is not of God.

Close your eyes right now and push all other thoughts aside. Imagine how pleasing you are to the Lord and how beautiful you are in His sight.

Look at the jewels on your breastplate, their shimmering glow reminding the Lord of His children. Perhaps one of those jewels is your daughter, son, husband, wife, or parent. Feel the warmth as the love from your own heart enwrap each jewel.

Now notice the onyx stones—those who are lost or are in a backslidden condition. Those who are held captive by Satan are enshrined in these pouches of gold. On your intercessory shoulders they will stay until, one by one, they are healed and put as a jewel upon your breastplate!

Once clothed in this magnificent, powerful garment, we will enter into the holy of holies and petition our King for His grace and mercy on our lives and the lives of those for whom we pray.

Chapter 12 ————————————

Preparing For Intercession

If the Spirit of God is within you, your spirit is the secret place—the dwelling place, the holy place—of the living God. You need not look for another:

> In Him—and in fellowship with one another—you yourselves also are being built up [into this structure] with the rest, to form a fixed abode (dwelling place) of God in (by, through) the Spirit—Ephesians 2:22 Amplified.

> Jesus said: "Behold, the kingdom of God is within you"—Luke 17:21.

The Bible also says the mature in Christ have "the mind of Christ" (1 Corinthians 2:16). Although the Spirit of God dwells within His children, it takes time to progressively know His heart and mind and to ultimately have our soul possessed by Him. If ever we reach a pinnacle where we think we understand all, we will be sadly disillusioned. In the *pinnacle of perfection to which Jesus will bring the faithful and diligent believer, God will in fact impart* the very mind of Christ through this lofty possession of the soul. It is a worthy goal to which we are called to aspire.

By studying the different parts of the tabernacle, we can gain great insight into God's care and love toward us as New Testament believers. It is because of His loving attitude, great mercy and responsive grace that we can enter His presence to pray.

In the book of Exodus, God gave the Israelites a pattern from which to build the tabernacle. Each room, piece of furniture, and utensil had a specific purpose and meaning in God's plan for communicating with His people.

I am not attempting to establish a ritualistic worship by suggesting the tabernacle as a format from which to work. You will find, however, that by following some simple procedures, your times of communion with the Lord will be less encumbered with striving. Your fellowship with Him will become more sacred as you allow the Holy Spirit to lead you into His presence.

THE CLEANSING PROCESS

Outside the holy place, where the Jews worshiped, stood the *brazen altar*. Imagine yourself standing before this altar, and let your heart grow full of God. Then begin to place your sacrifices on the altar. These are sacrifices of *self*—self-centeredness, self-pity, self-interest, self-display, self-motives, etc. Right now, stop reading, take whatever time is necessary, and let the Holy Spirit work in your heart. Ask Him to reveal anything unacceptable in you as you move inside the holy of holies.

Once while engaged in this part of my worship, the Lord revealed things about me of which I needed to repent. I went to the altar and wept. As I repented of each sin God was showing me, my heart filled up until it overflowed with a sweet feeling of love that permeated my being. This happened after each confession. Because of the uniqueness of the experience, I asked the Lord why He was so mercifully opening this to me.

Just then, I saw a vision replaying the entire experience between the Holy Spirit and me. I saw Jesus on the cross. As I repented of each sin, what seemed to be a liquid, would pour out of His heart to me. On each gushing stream was written the word "grace." As it touched my heart, I felt the sweetness of His love.

Jesus Christ deals with our repented sin by His grace. In Greek, *grace* means "the divine influence upon the heart and its reflection in the life." Once we accept the responsibility for our sin, God will pour out His generous grace upon us to begin the transforming influence.

Remember, any change the Lord wants to make in you is for your own good. Jesus bought you with His blood and cherishes you with His life.

Ephesians 5:29-32 says:

> No man ever hated his own flesh, but nourishes and carefully protects and cherishes it, as Christ does the church, because we are members (parts) of His body.... **The two shall become one flesh.** This mystery is very great, but I speak concerning [the relation of] Christ and the church—Amplified, bold italics added.

As a Christian, you are progressively becoming one with Jesus. He loves you tenderly and desires to nurture you. You never have to be afraid of this cleansing process or feel condemned as you admit your sins. Prayer is spiritual communion with our wonderful Lord. Jesus knows us much better than we can ever know ourselves, yet He loves us completely. Therefore, as the Holy Spirit reveals to you what you must place on the brazen altar, thank Him. Then let Him consume the offering with His fire.

It is upon this brazen altar that we also put our will and our rights. As a Christian we have only the right of godly brokenness. To live before God in this divine brokenness is to live a yielded life, having set aside our will and our rights to live in His own.

Jesus once came to me and took me to stand high upon a mountain with Him. I had been praying that He would give me the kind

149

of relationship with Him that He gave to Moses. So, as I stood before Him, I again stated my request. He only looked at me. He said nothing. This made me nervous, for Jesus looked like He was looking right through my very soul. I then realized that He wanted something I had not yet given to Him.

Feeling a little desperate, I looked around and noticed lying over to my right side were two ugly red rocks. These rocks were about the size that would fit into the palm of my hands. I walked over and picked them up, one in each hand, and turned to walk back to Jesus. As I did, I noticed standing to His side was a brazen altar. So, I walked over and laid the rocks upon the altar, looked at my Savior and said to Him: "Jesus, I give you my will and my rights as symbolized by these ugly red rocks. You can have them Lord!" Just then fire came down from heaven and consumed the rocks. Jesus smiled! I was then comforted with the promise that I could have my hearts desire.

To enter into completeness found only in Christ, we must be willing to give Him these two most important aspects of our person. If we come and daily place these valuables upon the brazen altar, we will come at length to find our full identity in Christ, having entered into our "Rest". If we do not lay these things upon the altar, although God will use us in prayer, we will never enter into the fullness of the overcoming life. The exchange is well worth the effort to make. His will for ours—His rights, that of the crucified life—for ours.

Next imagine yourself walking to the *laver of brass*. This laver was filled with water for the priests to wash their hands and feet. For you, however, it is the place to release the accumulation of the day's infirmities, including worries, fears, and misunderstandings. Give the Holy Spirit time to quicken things to you of which you may not be consciously aware.

It's often the little daily occurrences that mount up inside us and become the sources of emotional injury. Then this injury becomes integrated into our interactions with others.

During the process of cleansing, I am often shown things that need attention. A curt word, an unexpected phone bill, an ungodly worry or concern for a family member—all these things may pop up in my intimate time with God and interrupt our sweet fellowship. Releasing these hindrances to Him as soon as I am aware of them allows Him to wash me. Then I can enter in with a heart that's soft, tender, and ready to be led by the gentle Holy Spirit.

As the Lord reveals hidden sins or anxieties, thank Him for each thing He brings to your attention. Ask for His forgiveness, and tell Him how much you appreciate Him.

THE HOLY PLACE OF PRAISE

Then move toward the *holy place*, leaving outside its doors all that could possibly interfere in your time of communion and intercession with the Lord.

Once inside, approach the *showbread*. This is the table where you dine on His Word. Talk to the Lord, and express appreciation for His life-giving bread. Meditate on a scripture. Let it sink deep into your heart, giving the Holy Spirit time to bring enlightenment.

This is often the time when God will open His Word. It's this illumination of Scripture that changes my walk with Him or my relationships with other people. For example, one day the words *"a prudent man ignores an insult,"* (*Proverbs 12:16 Amplified*), came alive to me. The more I meditated upon that verse, the more I loved it and appreciated the freedom in it. I knew that at some point that day I would need its practical application.

I did—and the verbal barrage came from a most unexpected source. Normally, I would have to battle the desire to defend myself silently and justify my actions. But that day it was easy to walk away and ignore the insult. Later, I received a call of apology. There have been countless times since when I've wisely ignored an insult. Many times it has reaped great dividends in my relationships with people.

Meditation upon God's Word is so very important, not only for the comfort such as I just mentioned, but for communion with Jesus.

I remember a time many years ago, I was verbally attacked by someone who had misunderstood something I did. As a result of this attack, I was feeling very wounded inside. So, I went before the Lord. As I entered in to dine upon the showbread of His Word, Jesus began to open up to me the eighth chapter of Romans in a dimension I had never understood before. As I pondered and meditated upon it, it was as though heaven opened its very portals to me. Within a couple of hours, my heart was completely healed of the pain I had incurred.

Further, I have often experienced visions, trances, and visitations from the Lord during times of meditation upon His Word. As I am seeking His face about the meaning of the scripture, and when He has judged my sincerity of desire to be pure and my spirit is properly prepared for the new truth, He will visit me personally to give me the deep inner meaning of His Word.

How do we engage in true Biblical meditation? Locate a Scripture or a chapter of which you would like better understanding. Read it and ask the Lord what it means. Read all around it, perhaps even up to a couple chapters preceding or following the actual text of your choice. By this means seek to understand the Scripture in context. Then think about it from every angle in your mind. Again, ask the Holy Spirit to give you understanding of the Scripture. Then spend time waiting upon the Lord either silently, or softly praying in your prayer language, or softly singing in the spirit. Then start the whole process over again until the Lord reveals the deep inner meaning of the Scripture.

In 1997 I had again been thinking a great deal about our Lord's experience upon the cross, over a period of several weeks. Jesus appeared to me on the cross and revealed an aspect of the cross that I had not known before. I couldn't get this new insight out of my mind for days following the revelation. I kept asking Jesus what gave Him the ability and strength to endure. Was it His love for the Father, or for mankind? Or perhaps it was His Love for both. I continued asking Him this question until finally He spoke to me. He spoke audibly and tenderly saying: "It was My love for you that gave Me the strength to endure." Well, I wept and wept. I was feeling so loved by Him. Even now as I write this I weep again. It was a wonderful understanding of the Word that was well worth waiting for.

How I cherish these times of communion with God over His Word. But they should not preclude Bible study or personal time of devotions. Rather it should complement these times and add flavor to the banquet of His truth.

Chapter 13 ———————————

Worship In Spirit

PRAISE OF THE SPIRIT

When this "feast" is over, follow the Holy Spirit to the *golden candlestick*. Once again, consciously let the Holy Spirit flood you. Sense the peace and joy as your communion flows ever deeper. Then begin to praise Him, singing choruses of praise. Use your favorite scriptures or your own words, and make up your own melodies. Praise Him for all that He has given and done for you. Don't limit yourself or strive! Let the Holy Spirit lead as you enjoy the fellowship, and let it be a time of pure joy. When you have finished praising Him for what He has *done*, then praise Him for what He is *going to do*.

The Bible says: *"Enter his gates with thanksgiving and his courts with praise; give thanks to him and praise his name."* (Psalm 100:4 NIV). And again: *"I will praise God's name in song and glorify him with thanksgiving."* (Psalm 69:30 NIV).

This seems to be a difficult area for some saints because they feel they don't have a nice singing voice. I had the same problem in the beginning.

One night the Lord gave me an experience to teach me about praise. I found myself standing in a circle of saints on the earth.

Suddenly the Holy Spirit moved me into the middle of the group to lead in praise and worship. As our not-so-good voices rose to heaven, the song entered the gates—and was transformed. I was then taken up into heaven to take part in what was happening there. Our praise was so beautiful that a circle of angels began to gather in heaven to worship right above our circle.

Next, a second, larger circle gathered around the first group of angels, the inner circle singing in one heavenly language and the outer circle in another. There aren't words to describe what this heavenly choir sounded like. Mixed with our little earthly choir, their voices were filled with inexpressible joy. Jesus walked toward them, and their voices exploded into a rapture of joyous worship. He said that whenever we worship Him on earth, our praise is joined in heaven. I wept tears of joy. Since then, I haven't had a problem with my "not-so-good voice" as I worship the Lord.

Remembering all the good things He has done encourages my faith and lifts the Lord's heart. When I've gone through long storms, it's too easy to get trial-minded and problem-oriented. Daily refreshing, however, quickly puts a stop to that negative destructive cycle.

One year Melinda and I held a "tent revival" in Fresno. Working with several local pastors, we saw a great harvest of souls. One afternoon near the end of the meetings, one of the men had to get into the storage unit where the instruments and supplies were stored. Discovering a fifteen hundred-dollar unit missing, he phoned us immediately. Melinda called the insurance company and discovered she had forgotten to add that piece of equipment to the policy.

While Melinda panicked, I *praised*. Remembering all the good things God had done, I walked around the tent and praised Him for half an hour. Then I turned to Melinda and said: "God will come through." Within two days, just in time for the next service, God did come through. In a series of incidents, God glorified Himself not through one miracle but several. Once again He was praised for all the victories He had *already* given.

THE DANCE

There is another aspect of praise that I would like you to consider. That is the praise of the dance.

The Church has over the last couple of decades moved into "dancing before the Lord" as a means of expressing their praises unto God. This has come as a result of some well intended but erroneous teaching.

Jesus has dealt with me regarding this issue since 1990, but lately in some rather extreme ways. I suppose if I were to share all that He has given me regarding this issue it would comprise an entire book. So, I will simply share enough with you here to make the matter of His heart clear.

The Lord Himself said that the Father is looking for a people who would worship Him in *"Spirit and in truth"*, not in the flesh. He already had a nation of people worshipping Him in the flesh, and He was soon to bring that entire system to an end. It was a system to be set aside for it could not bring the worshipper to perfection in God. (Heb. 7:11,12; 8:13; 9:10) It therefore needed to be set aside for a new and better form of worship. This new worship would be in Spirit and in Truth. Paul listed the means by which we could express our praise and worship unto the Lord in the books of Ephesians, Colossians, and in Timothy. This includes singing psalms, hymns, and spiritual songs, and lifting up holy hands. By worshipping Jesus in psalms, we are given the privilege of worshipping Him with musical instruments. It does not however include dancing before the Lord, using banners or flags. Nor does it include applauding Jesus for any reason. All these are of the flesh, a system which as been done away with for the sake of the higher. To continue to worship Jesus by this means is equivalent to, in the Old Testament, worshipping Him by building our own altar of hewn stones rather than a humble altar of rocks according to the Lord's desire.

The Lord understands that the Church has engaged in this form of praise thinking that it is pleasing to Him. But, it is not. For the flesh profits nothing. Only what is done by the spirit is of any value.

Recently in a service, where I was to minister later that evening, we were in a time of worship. People were dancing before the Lord, some even parading children in a train across the sanctuary. Others were waving banners and flags before the Lord. I was in my own little world however. I desired to worship Jesus in spirit. I, at one point went down to my knees to enter into deeper worship trying hard to ignore the commotion around me. At last I was able to enter such a deep and intimate time of worship that it felt like Jesus was standing right in front of me. As I later prepared to stand, I opened my eyes and found Jesus standing right there in front of me. I stood up, so I could see Him face to face. He turned slightly pointing at all those who were dancing, and softly but intently cried: "Look at what they are doing. Nita, do you see what they are doing? They are taking glory that belongs only to the Father". He then gave me a vision of myself cleansing the temple just like Jesus did as is recorded in the book of John. The difference being that instead of the Lord being wrapped in a furious and divine zeal, it was me. I was cleansing the temple of the dancers. Jesus had tears gently flowing down His bronze face as we talked. He then let me feel His hurt, and the grief He was experiencing over the scene that lay before us.

I was by now stunned and in pain myself. Further, the fear of the Lord was upon me. So, I felt desperate to obey Him in cleansing the temple. Jesus spoke for a few more minutes then left, leaving behind Him a twirling and flaming sword that stood the size of a man, where He was once standing. The pastor was a short distance away from me worshipping the Lord and the assistant pastor was in the back of the church wrapped in the fear of the Lord, as he lay upon his face. I immediately went over and asked the pastor to stop the dancers, to which he agreed. I told him that the Lord is lifting His glory from the church because of the dancing in the flesh. He replied: "I know." He then stepped forward and brought it to an end. The pastor later told me that just seconds before I came up to him to ask him to clear out the dancers, he himself felt the presence of the Lord leave. At the same moment the assistant pastor in the back of the room felt the presence of the Lord leave. It took some time of repentance before the presence of the Lord returned. When He did return, it was with a much higher manifestation of His presence.

As I have traveled and shared the Lord's heart on this matter, it seems that those churches that have complied with His wish and discontinued the dancing in the flesh, are now starting to receive various new levels of the Lord's glory in their services. His presence is a new and exciting expression of Himself to His people .

I am often confronted on the issue of the dancing before the Lord that David did. As a result, I sought the Lord and meditated on it. One morning Jesus gave me a vision of the whole thing.

David had gathered his elders, priests and mighty men together to bring up the Ark of God. He had by now recovered from the trauma of Uzza's death and was determined to bring the Ark to Jerusalem the right way. As the parade started, being now officiated according to the dictates of the Lord, God's blessings were very apparently upon them. When David realized this, he was greatly humbled and thankful. As David humbled himself, I saw a beam of lightening shoot from heaven straight into David's heart. It was God's own humility. When this occurred, David commanded that the caravan stop and offer sacrifices to the Lord. After the sacrifices had been offered David was so happy, that it opened His heart to receive from the Lord again. I then saw another shaft of light shoot down from heaven right into David's soul. It was the joy and glory of the Lord. When this glory exploded in David, it set his feet a dancing, and he danced, some say nine miles, all the way into Jerusalem. He danced the dance of the Spirit. After seeing this I asked the Lord about Miriam and the ladies after the Exodus. The Lord told me it was the same thing. God did the same thing in Miriam as He had in David as a celebration of His purpose for Israel.

Again, the Lord knows that the Church believes they are pleasing Him with this dance of the flesh, so He is not angry, but He is grieved, and He wants to help us. So, if we really want to please Him, we will discontinue the dance of the flesh, and wait for the dance of the Spirit.

The positive by product of saving ourselves for the dance of the Spirit is that growth will occur. Whenever we worship Jesus in the Spirit instead of the flesh, growth occurs. So, it will turn out to be a much higher blessing.

There is also a clap which is of the Spirit. But it is not to applaud the Lord. He doesn't need our applause, He wants our worship. When we feel a desire to applaud the Lord, if instead we will worship Him by lifting up holy hands in praise, He will bless us with a wonderful response.

I do not always enter into prayer by the means I have just mentioned, as I now walk more in an ever-living prayer which is all but constant. Notwithstanding, I do still enjoy times of sweet communion by means of the tabernacle which, I have shared with you.

So praise Him. Let heaven join in—and enjoy yourself!

WORSHIP: THE FINAL PREPARATION

Now imagine moving to the *golden altar*. Positioned right in front of the *holy of holies*, this altar was full of hot coals. As the high priest burned incense on these coals, the cloud of fragrance rising up before the mercy seat brought a sweet-smelling savor to the Lord.

This is the place where praise becomes worship. Here you will begin to worship the Lord for *Who* He is, not for *what* He has done. You will worship Him because He is God, Creator and Ruler of the universe and all that is—His might, His Power, and His unending love.

Sing in the spirit and also with words of understanding. Worship Him until your heart overflows with love and adoration. You may find yourself going in cycles. That's alright, too. Worship acts like palm branches that welcome the King into your presence.

You may reach peaks, at which time you will desire to fall into silence before Him: *"To You belongs silence [the submissive wonder of reverence which bursts forth into praise]"* (Psalm 65:1 Amplified). So don't be concerned. Be silent, and let His wonder fill your heart. Incidentally, this is the highest form of worship. The Lord may choose this time to talk to you.

During one of these times of silence, the Lord told me that He would *"make a way in the wilderness and rivers in the desert"* (Isaiah 43:19 Amplified).

One day we went to Yosemite in California. We were still high in the mountains, about half an hour from the valley, when the axle arm broke on the car. With a sudden thud, the car came to a halt inches from the side of the mountain. With the Scripture that the Lord had given me earlier tucked away in my heart, I said, "Well, this looks like a good opportunity to praise Him!"

Within a short time, a ranger came by and stopped to help. He was amazed that the car hadn't gone over the cliff. The way the axle arm broke, he said, it should have gone over. That was a perfect opportunity to share Jesus. Although the ranger listened and drank it all in, he wasn't quite ready to say yes. But a seed was planted.

After making the necessary arrangements to get the car to a station, the ranger gave us a ride. Once we were at the station, we needed to get the car towed back to Fresno. I made some calls and found a man who was the uncle of a dear friend of ours. I recognized his name because I had been praying for his salvation for nearly a year.

After he arrived and hooked up the car we all jumped in to head back home—a two-hour trip. As we started down the mountain range, I knew in my heart that today was going to be his day to make Jesus Christ Lord of his life.

The three of us talked for awhile, and then we led him in the sinner's prayer. Crying like a baby he shared about dreams he had been having for the last year about asking Jesus into his heart. Each day after having a dream like that, he would be happy all day long. He concluded that it was no longer a dream—Jesus was truly in his heart!

When we finally arrived home, he graciously reduced the towing bill. As he handed us the bill I thought, 'Now, where is the money to cover this and the extensive repair job on the car going to come from?' I remembered what the Lord had spoken that morning. He had already made a way in the wilderness and streams in the desert with the new soul born into the kingdom. Now we were facing a new wilderness, but I was confident that God would provide.

Before I could even get concerned, we were told that the car repair would be covered under a special clause in the warranty. My sister Valerie called to tell me that she and her husband had been praying about what to do with some extra money they had to give to the Lord. "This morning," she said: "the Lord spoke to both of us that we were to give it to you."

As she handed me the check, it turned out to be exactly the same amount as the reduced bill for towing the car. How glad I was that I had given the Holy Spirit time to talk to me in worship that morning.

There is another aspect of this that we need to consider as well. True worship brings revelation and spiritual growth. For instance, during a particularly difficult storm which lasted for several months, I constantly felt very needy of the Lord.

He took this opportunity to daily reveal His glory. During my times of worship, He would visit me in His visible glory and reveal different aspects of His nature and character. I would always become so overwhelmed that I would just fall on my face and weep with my heart brimming with love for Him. He would lift me up and draw me unto Himself and then let me experience that part of Himself that He had just revealed to me. This went on for weeks. By this means He caused me to grow in Himself. When this season came to an end, I had entered a new level of maturity.

Bask in the Holy Spirit, and delight yourself in worshipping your King. When the Holy Spirit chooses, He will move you on.

This is the last stop before the *holy of holies*. By the time you enter, you will be fully saturated by the Holy Spirit and ready to enter God's divine presence in intercession.

Chapter 14 —————————————————————

The Art Of Intercession

In chapter eleven we learned that Christ was *"clad with zeal as a cloak" (Isaiah 59:17)*. The word zeal in Hebrew means "fire," "to be fervent," or "to be so hot as to boil or glow." We also learned that we are now adorned with the same cloak—the ephod.

Although Jesus was clad in zeal and prayed earth-shaking prayers, the earth didn't actually shake beneath His feet when He prayed. Fire didn't consume everything in sight, even though He is a consuming fire. As He spoke under the unction of the Holy Spirit, He didn't seem to change much at all.

But Jesus Christ rocked the heavens and shook hell at its hinges. The evidence was manifested in the physical realm when He calmed the sea by prayer, healed thousands, brought the dead back to life, and transformed the world for thousands of years to follow. Jesus Christ was and still is the very epitome of an intercessor.

Two friends of mine, the late Wil and Gerdie Riedt, were well known for their ministry in intercession. Until they went to be with the Lord, they traveled throughout the world teaching on prayer. Wil said Gerdie always prayed silently, but he wasn't boisterous himself. I have stayed in their home many times, but I have never been disturbed by Wil's praying, although he gets up before the sun to intercede before the Lord.

Another friend named Shirley Moore is one of my most faithful prayer warriors. She is tenacious but quiet as she seeks God. Shirley grabs hold of the horns of the altar and doesn't let go until her answer comes. To watch her pray is beautiful—no show, just a child before her Father. But when Shirley prays, God listens!

Noise and animation don't make prayer profitable. It's the power of the Holy Spirit that brings results in prayer.

At times, however, prayer *can* be noisy and animated. A minister by the name of Dr. Michael Brown told me about the first time he prayed in a spirit of travail. No one had told him about such a thing, so he didn't know what hit him as he rolled around the floor in travail, groaning like he was having a baby. It didn't take him long to find out that it was the Holy Spirit, and he has since become used to this type of intercession.

The key in any type of prayer is that *as the Holy Spirit leads,* we must follow. If you want a successful prayer life, *let go and let God.* He will guide you.

The effectual fervent prayer of a righteous man availeth much—James 5:16.

The above scripture could read, "A prayer of a just man wrought in him by divine energy releases tremendous power of force—enough to prevail." Learning how a scripture was written in the original Greek can unlock rich nuggets of understanding. A brief study of this particular verse opens wide the gates of freedom in intercession.

Some people think that "effectual fervent prayer" means crying, shouting, screaming, yelling, shaking, pleading—anything that sounds good and fervent and makes you look spiritual. That, however, is *not* what it means at all.

"Effectual fervent prayer" simply means that if the Holy Spirit is in charge of the prayer, He will give more than enough power to get the job done. So, as we have said many times, let the Holy Spirit lead.

DIFFERENT WAYS TO PRAY

Ephesians 6:17 says: *"Take the helmet of salvation and the sword the Spirit wields, which is the Word of God."* (*Amplified*)

The Bible says that *the Spirit* wields the Word. We speak it, but it's the *inherent power* of the Word, which is the Spirit, that gets the job done. The Word is like a guided missile. You shoot it out, and the "sonar" locks in on the target—the enemy. He can dodge and serpentine all he wants, but he cannot avoid the missile of the Word once it locks onto him. When it hits, you win and Satan loses.

The Word is also our shield of faith—like a force field. The more you speak the Word, walking in faith and love, the higher and thicker the force field grows, until it's impenetrable. Unlike an old Roman shield, it covers all of you, not just the front. As you use the Word daily, you're protected from the enemy's flaming missiles in every direction. In this, then, we see that the Word is both our offensive weapon—a sword—and our defense—a shield.

The Word of God will energize you. Sometimes when I'm feeling weary from overwork, I begin to speak the Word—not necessarily scriptures on strength but just the Word in general—and my energy picks right up. I call it an "energy break."

In these days of the outpouring of the Holy Spirit, we "charismatics" sometimes overlook a powerful weapon while searching for a spiritual arsenal. I'm referring to *praying in our native tongue.*

In Genesis 18:23-32, Abraham interceded for Sodom and Gomorrah in his native tongue. Like Abraham, we have God's open ear. When we speak to Him as a friend, we don't have to be eloquent or lengthy, just honest and to the point.

One time a lady asked me to pray for her runaway husband. This man would move his family from one end of the United States to the other, only to leave them and get a job someplace else. After spending several months at his new location, he would send for them. Then he would move again without them to another job. The cycle repeated itself over and over. In fact, he had just left for another new job with a hotel chain when his wife called me. She was at her wit's end.

I prayed that the owner of the company would meet the husband at the airport and hand him a ticket for a return flight with an apology for not being able to hire him after all. I knew this would take God's intervention because the husband had quite a reputation for success in his field.

A few hours later, the wife received a call from her irate husband, who was on his way home. The president and board members of the hotel chain had met him at the airport with return tickets and an apology for not being able to hire him.

When he arrived home, she couldn't help but chuckle as she told her husband how I had prayed.

God obviously wanted the man to settle down, for He had answered the prayer precisely.

Obviously, the other side of the coin is to *pray in tongues*. The Holy Spirit knows much more about the intricacies of situations and needs than we do. When we release Him to pray through us—uninhibited by our natural understanding—more can be accomplished—and faster.

In a church service on the west coast, the leader asked me to pray for a lady who was unable to walk. After introducing myself, I began to pray for her in tongues. As I did, she started weeping. When I asked her why she was crying, she told me in broken English that I had spoken in perfect Portuguese. The Holy Spirit had spoken this message through me: "I'm Jesus. I've come to save your soul and heal your body."

Without hesitation, she gave her heart to Jesus Christ, got up, and walked—totally healed! When the Holy Spirit called her by name in her own language, this woman's faith was lifted to receive what she needed from God.

Once while I was staying with Wil and Gerdie Riedt, the Lord called me to prayer. At the time, I was fellowshipping with some friends; but the Spirit bade, and I had to go.

Stepping outside into the backyard, I prayed in tongues for about an hour. I finally asked the Lord why I was praying. As I did, I noticed some fruit trees in the Riedt's backyard. Suddenly, I saw white rain falling down on the trees. I went over to see if I could feel it, I walked all over the small orchard, but not a drop hit me. Returning to the yard to eye it from a distance, I saw, sure enough, that white rain was falling onto the fruit trees.

I asked the Lord what He was trying to tell me, and He said, "You're watering My trees of righteousness with your prayer." This excited me so much that I received the strength to pray another hour.

SINGING AND LAUGHING

At times, we may be moved to sing prayer-songs of deliverance. The Bible says:

> Sing to God, sing praises to His name; cast up a highway for Him who rides through the deserts; His name is the Lord, be in high spirits and glory before Him—Psalm 68:4 Amplified.
>
> You, Lord, preserve me from trouble; You surround me with songs and shouts of deliverance—Psalm 32:7 Amplified .

I have ministered in *songs of deliverance* on a few different occasions. Once while demonstrating this to an audience, I sang over a lady's back and stomach. When I finished, she started laughing as she told the audience that she had come into the service with a terrible backache and stomachache. Now both were gone.

Husbands and wives should sing over one another each morning before they start their day. You'll be surprised at the difference it will make. I have taught this in many places across the country and have received reports of the good things it has brought into the lives of many families.

One of the most unusual forms of powerful prayer is *laughter*. Psalm 2:4 says: "*He that sitteth in the heavens shall laugh: the Lord shall have them in derision.*"

While driving across the state of Nebraska after a week of meetings, I was in prayer for a teenage girl who was bound by a drug habit. After I had prayed for almost six hours, a strange thing happened. I suddenly began to laugh so hard that tears came to my eyes. I laughed and laughed and laughed. As I did, I knew that the girl had been set free of Satan's hold.

About a month later, I found out this troubled teenager had been set free from her drug addiction that very day. Laughter too, may be a powerful weapon when anointed by the Holy Spirit.

TRAVAILING IN PRAYER

Many times you may feel a deep concern for a person or a certain situation, yet you are not sure what you should pray *for*. In Scripture we read:

> *The Spirit also helpeth our infirmities: for we know not what we should pray for as we ought: but the Spirit itself maketh intercession for us with groanings which cannot be uttered*—Romans 8:26.

The word "helpeth" in Greek is *sunantilambanomai*. It suggests a picture of the Holy Spirit coming and putting His arm around us to be our strength, while at the same time fighting off the enemy of our soul.

The words "maketh intercession," which in Greek is one word—*huperentugchano*—is a picturesque work of rescue. It gives the visualization of a person coming to rescue a drowning man. In short, the Spirit takes up the battle we can't fight and powers forth to victory on our behalf.

When this type of war is waged in us by the Holy Spirit, our only prayer may be groanings in the Spirit. It may come as a deep, throaty groan—one you might give as you try to shove your foot into a tight boot. If your groaning is greater for a greater need, it may come from your stomach—like a sound you would make if you had a bad stomachache. The difference is that you're giving Satan a stomachache!

> *Who has heard such a thing? Who has seen such things? Shall a land be born in one day? Or shall a nation be brought forth in a moment? For as soon as Zion was in **labor** she brought forth her children.*—Isaiah 66:8 *Amplified,* bold italics added.

> *Elijah went up to the top of Carmel; and he cast himself down upon the earth, and put his face between his knees*—1 Kings 18:42.

This is a "birthing" prayer, or travail. The apostle Paul said: "My little children, of whom I travail in birth again until Christ be formed in you." (Galatians 4:19).

As this spirit of intercession comes over you, you will feel compelled to enter the "birthing position" in which Elijah prayed. You may feel as if you are giving birth to a baby—and you are! You're birthing a spiritual baby, whether it's making the way for a soul to enter the Kingdom of God or praying forth a new ministry.

As you pray, you will feel like you're in labor. The closer you get to delivery, the harder the pains in your bowel area will be, and you will groan like a woman in labor. The travail will flow in rhythm, growing in intensity and then subsiding—only to grow again until the spiritual work is complete.

I have seen many ministries birthed throughout the country as a result of this type of prayer. Once I was praying in this fashion, and the Lord gave me a vision of a baby in the birth canal. Each time I prayed about or ministered in relation to this work I would travail, and the Lord would give me another vision of the baby getting closer and closer to the time of birth.

The last time I travailed, the vision showed that the baby had been born. That night during a worship service the wind of the Holy Spirit came in—just like in the second chapter of Acts—and no one could stand under His power.

TEARS OF INTERCESSION

Another form of intercession is *the weeping prayer*. Jeremiah was no stranger to this type of praying. He cried out:

> *Behold, O Lord, how distressed I*
> *am! My vital parts are in tumult,*
> *my heart cannot rest and is violent-*
> *ly agitated within me .... My eyes*
> *fail from weeping, my emotions are*
> *deeply disturbed, my heart is*
> *poured out upon the ground in*
> *grief] —* Lamentations 1:20, 21
> *Amplified.*

The purpose for this weeping is obvious. In this prayer, you feel God's agony as well as the agony of the one for whom you're inter-ceding. It is a prayer that truly lets you feel the love of God poured out.

The apostle Paul said: *"I shall bewail many which have sinned already."* (2 Corinthians 12:21).

The deepest kind of intercession, called *bewailing prayer*, is begotten of the Spirit, born of love, and comes with a wailing cry of grief. The love that flows through this prayer is so deep that you will feel as though you will die if the need isn't met. Your burden will be so great that you would pour your innermost soul over hell to protect the object of your prayer.

In this spirit of intercession—and this one alone—you will feel the agape love that Christ walked in and which made Him give His life for us. You will want, with all your might, to do the same during this travail. I wish everyone in the church would experience this kind of prayer. If so, hell would be deprived of the world and we would see the biggest evangelistic move the world has ever seen. The door of hell would be blown off its hinges as Satan goes reeling head over heels.

MORE TYPES OF INTERCESSION

As you grow and mature in the things of the Spirit, the Lord will begin to let you experience other forms of intercession such as those I am about to mention. A Christian might occasionally experience these in their earlier experiences. But, to be used in this manner on a regular basis is reserved for the more mature.

WRESTLING WITH PRINCES

Any believer can take authority over evil spirits in the name of Jesus. For everything is subject to that name. And, as a Christian you operate under a delegated authority. But, the Lord usually leaves dealing with principalities to those who are anointed to deal with them.

As I travel from church to church, I always leave myself open to hearing from the Lord as to what evil spirit is hindering the various works with which I come into contact. When it is time to reveal the spirit that has been commissioned to destroy the work that God is doing in a given area, Jesus will remove the spiritual veil and let me see who I am dealing with. There are times however, that the greatest   problem has not come from a prince over a church, but a much higher ruling prince over a city or even false religion. Let me give you an example.

One time while ministering in the Hawaiian Islands, I flew over to a smaller Island to speak. As I entered the pastor's home the spirit of travail came upon me. So I promptly went to my room to pray. Immediately upon entering a place of privacy, I was lifted up off the earth and taken to a place in the heavens being brought face to face with Aligar, the ruling spiritual monarch over the world wide Catholic Church.

His appearance is best described by comparing him with the Himalayan bigfoot. He stands upright like a man, and is covered with brown fur like a bear. His face is leathery like a monkey but shaped a little more like a man's. His hands are shaped like a bear's with long talons. As I looked at him I knew who it was as I had been face to face with him in the past. Over his head were the words: "the spirit of compromise." On his chest were the words: "The Beast."

I saw him guiding and controlling the souls of men throughout the world. As I saw him leading them to the mouth of hell, I became enraged, and cried out: "Aligar, release your captives!" Well the war began. We wrestled for nearly 45 minutes. When I completed my task, I was brought back to my room. Later in the service, I saw many souls released from his idolatries. (Dan. ch. 10; Eph. 6:12) This is a type of warfare that is done face to face with the principalities. A person could never engage in such warfare without permission from the Holy Spirit. But when He approves, you are protected by a supernatural faith, and most assured of victory.

OVER THE NATIONS

There are times when God will use accomplished intercessors to intercede over the nations at a higher level wherein, He will lift you up over the nation for which you are interceding. Once while ministering in Kansas, I was lifted up and carried over the United States. I flew from the west coast to the east coast. As I did, I was viewing America in the future. The land was blighted and ravaged by war and draught. I couldn't believe my eyes. I was horrified by what I was seeing everywhere. I wept and wept before the Lord, in deep intercession, pleading for my country. (Ezk. 8:3)

Indeed America will experience what I saw that day. My prayer now is that the body of Christ will be ready.

WEEPING WITH JESUS

Another of the higher forms of intercession is to weep with Jesus face to face, here on earth.

While ministering in Australia recently, we had a service that was predominately intercession. At one point, I looked up and saw the nation's capital building. I looked to the right of the building and saw my Savior walking toward it. I asked Him what He was doing. He turned and looked at me and said; "Watch!" Then He knelt down and bowed Himself over the building like a mother over her little child and began to weep profusely before the Father. After a while He turned to me again and said: "Tell My people to weep with Me." Immediately I fell into deep tears of grief as I too wept before the Father, over Australia. (Gen. 19) I have wept with Jesus like this many times over people, churches, and nations.

BEFORE THE THRONE

I suppose one could say this is the highest of all intercessions. I had been in prayer for about an hour, when suddenly I was lifted up to stand before the judgment seat of Christ! Jesus was sitting on His throne, and standing between us was the Spirit of Judgment. My Lord did not at all look pleased. Therefore, I was terribly frightened by the sight of Him. The terror and holiness of God was emanating from the Spirit of Judgment, which further terrified me.

Jesus then spoke to me saying: "I have brought you here to speak to you about three people upon which I am going to bring judgment." As He spoke to me, He spoke about one person at a time. After He would tell me what He was going to do, I felt compelled to intercede for them that He would delay His judgment and grant them another season of mercy.

When Jesus was comforted by my intercession He would relent, and promise another season of mercy, as I requested. My pleadings were literally one word at a time, slow and carefully thought out. For I feared the Spirit of judgment being released upon me.

When we came to the third party, I found myself offering my own life if He would just give mercy a little longer to the object of my prayers. I knew that if Jesus accepted my offer, that I would be the one who would fall under the wrath of this dreadful and holy Spirit that stood in front of me. Yet, I feared it would take that kind of pleading to turn the Lord's heart to one of mercy, so I continued.

At long last, Jesus was comforted, and He relented, giving another season of mercy to that soul as well. My life was spared as well for He could never have accepted my offer in His holiness. When my intercessions were complete, I was comforted and filled with His peace. (Amos ch.7 and Ex. 33:13-17)

My daughter tells of a time when she was in intercession for a church in which I was ministering. As she went to her knees, she found herself suddenly before the Lord's throne.

She interceded for the church; then the Lord gave her a fourfold promise for the church, then returned her to her living room.

Many are the wonderful experiences that await the true and sincere seeker, and faithful intercessor. So, press into God through prayer, with full abandon. You will never be sorry. This completes the section on various forms of intercession. I trust that the encouragements I have offered will help you on your way. As you are faithful in the least, Jesus will increase you and advance you to the higher forms of prayer.

DELIVERANCE FROM BONDAGE

To close this chapter, let's look at the way God worked through one of His mightiest intercessors.

Moses was commissioned by God to deliver Israel from Egypt. As Moses answered the call, God methodically stripped away all the hindrances standing in his way before deliverance came. Let's look at how He accomplished that.

First, the Bible teaches that behind every idol worshiped is a demon: *"They sacrificed unto devils, not to God"* (*Deuteronomy 32:17*). Each miracle Moses performed was an act of judgment against those ruling demons.

God said to Moses:

> *I am the Lord, and I will bring you out from under the burdens of the Egyptians, and I will rid you out of their bondage, and I will redeem you with a stretched out arm, and with great* **judgments**—Exodus 6:6, bold italics added.

As each demon was judged, its power over the people was broken, thereby ultimately bringing freedom to the Israelites and many Egyptians.

Let's look further at the process of deliverance and learn what we must do to free those for whom we are praying.

First Moses saw the need—Israel's freedom; second, he asked the Lord what to do about it; third, the Lord gave him specific directives; fourth, Moses obeyed each command precisely; fifth, He then gave the captives (Israel) orders; sixth, they obeyed; seventh, the people were delivered.

Let's say you deeply desire someone you love to come to Christ. How do you make this type of "deliverance" from darkness happen?

The first thing you need to do is ask the Lord what spirit is hindering this process. Perhaps He will say it's the spirit of fear. Start praying against the spirit of fear, binding its power over that person. Do this every day until you feel the demonic power has been broken. The Lord may give you a special form of intercession, such as weeping prayer or travail to break its power.

You may have to come against several spiritual forces before you get the victory. It could take months or even years. Just as the Israelites still had Pharaoh to consider after the plagues, you will still have to deal with the will of the person after all the blinding spirits are broken. But continued prayer can gain the victory.

Once everything is broken, the person for whom you are praying may need to take a step of obedience to be totally free. Maybe they will have to give up cigarettes or another binding habit.

Israel who had been redeemed by the blood of the passover lamb had to take a difficult step of obedience. These poor beaten down slaves had to go to their oppressors and ask for riches. Think how hard that would be to do.

If there is a final step of obedience for them to take, God will tell you. But don't be presumptuous; ask the Lord if there is anything you have missed or if any habits must be broken. If you have completely done your job in prayer, your "spiritual patient" will be ready to do just what is needed. You will have won your war!

The principles are the same for any object of prayer whether it is for salvation, a business need, birthing a ministry, setting someone free of sickness, praying your congregation into the things of God or the unity and healing of a family. You can even help set a community, city, state, or nation free from Satan's hold using these principles. You persist; *God* will win the war.

Chapter 15————————————

The Life Of Prayer

Many people ask: "How do I know when the Holy Spirit is calling me to pray?" Because Scripture issues a continuous call to prayer, we need no emotional urges to be faithful in our communication with God. However, many of us have experienced urgent impressions from the Holy Spirit that direct us to intercede for a specific situation. This chapter will cover those specific promptings, but does not overlook our call to a continuous devotional life.

In this final chapter, we will look at some simple and basic ways to recognize the tug of the Holy Spirit. The more you lend yourself to following His call, the more sensitive you will become. And the more you prove your obedience, the more He will use you. So, first set in your heart the *determination of obedience*, like an immovable mountain. It will take this kind of commitment, as the enemy will try his best to steer you off course.

Primarily, you may experience such *a strong, sudden yearning for God* in the pit of your stomach or in your heart that you will feel compelled to pray. It will still take your obedience, however, since it is quite easy to make excuses and go about your business. If you do ignore the burden, God will have to use another intercessor, and you will lose the joy of being used by Him.

One day I was ironing a blouse to wear to a service that night when suddenly I felt an urgency to pray. Turning off the iron, I went into the living room. By the time I reached the sofa, I was weeping intensely. Suddenly I received a vision of the man who was to minister in our tent crusade that night. Sensing that he was having a heart attack and that an evil spirit was seeking to quench his physical life, I travailed in prayer for forty-five minutes before I felt victorious.

Later, when he and his wife arrived at the tent, I asked them about it. The wife replied casually, "Well, Howard started to have chest pains on the way to the meeting, but I prayed a simple prayer of faith. As you can see, he is fine now."

All I could do was smile. She had no idea of the forty-five minute wrestling match with spiritual forces that lay behind her "simple" prayer.

Another call to intercession may actually come in the form of *a sudden ailment in your body.*

Although this has happened to me many times, one occasion stands out in particular.

I was ministering with a friend on the east coast. We were conducting a series of meetings at a church in Baltimore and had a few days to prepare for an upcoming meeting in Pennsylvania.

As I began my work at the church in Baltimore my heart began to hurt, as in an angina attack. Somehow I knew my heart wasn't defective but that I was to intercede for another. For three days the pain persisted, and for three days I prayed without ceasing. On the way to our next church in Pennsylvania, I finally realized I had been interceding for the pastor.

When we arrived at the church, I inquired about his health. Sure enough, a heart attack had nearly taken his life. The doctors couldn't understand why he made it through, but we soon discovered that the Lord had raised up intercessors all over the nation. Calls had been streaming in from faithful prayer warriors for days. Prayer had pulled him through .

DEPRESSION AND ANXIETY

Gerdie Reidt told me of a time when she came under a terrible depression. Not given to such moods, Gerdie sensed it was an intercessory call. So she prayed for three days. On the third day, the Lord told her for whom she had been interceding.

When Gerdie called the woman to tell her what had transpired, the woman burst into tears. She had just come through the worst three days of her life and said that it took every bit of strength she could muster not to commit suicide. But, praise God, the depression had lifted that day.

General feelings of anxiety—not depression but anxiety of the heart—can also be a call to intercede.

One spring morning, I woke up with such a heavy anxiety that I could hardly walk. I forced myself, however, to go for a walk around the nearby lake to pray. The minute I stepped onto the lone country road, I burst into tears. I knew this anxiety, which seemed to rip at my very bowels, was over my daughter Ricci. The work in prayer now completed, I returned home in joy and called her.

Surprised and excited by my call, Ricci told me that she had felt an unbearable brokenness and cried out to God in that very hour for His mercy. The attack had suddenly subsided, and the burden she was under broke. A Christian friend stopped by to take her to lunch, and they talked and laughed. She said: "Mom, I don't know what I would have done if God hadn't helped me. But I'm doing great now!"

Sometimes I will feel lonely for someone. It will be as if their face is ever before me. When this happens, I know they need prayer.

Melinda and I were ministering in Indianapolis when this feeling came over me for my sister, Marci. Everyone seemed to remind me of my sister, and with every thought of her I started to cry.

After the meetings ended, I called Marci and discovered she had a tumor that needed immediate surgery. After we cried together, I told her to wait a few days because we would be traveling near her home in Michigan. I knew God was going to heal her.

After I arrived, we prayed together, and the Lord did heal her. We spent some quality time together and both felt refreshed when I left.

Generally, I don't feel a need to go to the one who needs intercession, but in this case it was necessary. God may call you to do the same.

DREAMS AND VISIONS

One vivid way God may call you to prayer is through a *dream or a vision*. One night when my daughter was in her teens, I had a terrible dream that she had been killed. Startled and shaken, I arose and prayed the rest of the night. Later that day, my sister Valerie called with the news that an attempt had been made on Ricci's life. The store where she was working had been held up. The man had just cocked the trigger of his gun in Ricci's face when, unexpectedly, a customer came in. In panic, the thief took off running. Ricci's life was spared because I prayed!

Similarly, you may experience sleeplessness.

I was once ministering in Georgia. It was quite late and I was laying awake unable to sleep at all, so I began to pray. The next thing I knew, I was being visited by a heavenly ambassador. He came to give me a message about a critical situation and the answer to the existing problem. After he left, I was immediately visited by a high satanic prince in the area. I wasn't too delighted in seeing him, as I had dealt with this guy before. But, we had a brief confrontation after which he left, and I saw another spirit sitting upon the church in which I was ministering. I asked him what he was doing sitting on top of that church. His reply was that the prince I had just confronted had ordered him to destroy the work of God in the church. Needless to say, I canceled his assignment, after which he left. It turned out to be a very busy night.

I have learned that when nights become sleepless it is frequently a call to pray, and sometimes even to urgent intercession.

God has many other ways of calling His children to prayer. I've told you only a few. The important thing is to be *faithful* in all that He calls you to do. The more faithful you are, the more He will use you.

PRAYER LISTS

I have saved this next category for last because it is the most evident, and I want to spend some time considering it. Sometimes we can overlook the *obvious need*.

Although I don't believe in governing your devotional life with a prayer list, they have their place. The benefit of having such a list is that you can spend five minutes an hour throughout the day praying for things on your prayer list. You can take one or two requests at a time and intercede by speaking the Word into situations and thanking the Lord for His gracious answers to your prayers. In twelve hours, that adds up to an hour of prayer.

These brief periods of intercession should never preclude your concentrated time alone with the Lord; rather, it should complement your personal prayer time.

John Wesley's mother raised more than a dozen children, kept house, cooked meals, chopped fire wood, went shopping, made all her children's clothes, and remained active in her community. But every day from noon until one o'clock she prayed. *Nothing* interfered with that hour with God. As a result of her faithfulness, she birthed powerful ministries in two of her sons.

PRAYER DIRECTIVES

Our prayer lists should include the following special needs:

1. World Governments

2. National Governments
3. Local Governments
4. Schools and Colleges (Secular and Christian)
5. Renowned leaders of the Body of Christ
6. Local leaders of the Body of Christ
7. The saints (worldwide)
8. Your family
9. The lost
10. Fullness of Pentecost
11. Israel
12. Continued peace between America and Israel. (The Lord told me in a dream that if America turned from Israel it would be to her demise.)

We should also pray every day for:

• The knowledge of things to come and the wisdom to overcome

• Your own walk with God to be rich and full

• Illumination of the Scriptures and a new love

PRAYING TO CHANGE DESTINY

While leaders of the church should be in prayer for the sheep under their care, it is not the responsibility of these leaders to do *all* the praying. God's leaders are His front-line soldiers, and they need to be supported by those who are behind them. Instead of judging God's leaders, we should be praying for them.

The same is true for our government leaders; we are *commanded* in the Word to pray for them. If we don't, we have no one to blame but ourselves if our nation is not going God's way. We have the power of God at our disposal to lead this country in His direction.

Recently, the Lord convicted me that we, the Church, need to pray in an unprecedented way for our national leaders. We are to pray that God will be able to move Christians of high caliber into government and that our defense system be greatly increased. Also, we are to pray America into repentance to stay the famine that is coming to our land.

Will we do it? Do we want to suffer the consequences of our lethargy if we don't?

The Lord gave me a vision of America swept clean—the country looked like a desert. War and famine had stripped our nation bare. I wept until I thought I would die. I asked the Lord why He was showing me the vision. He said: "The Church has forsaken the land."

The Bible says:

> *If my people, which are called by my name, shall humble themselves, and pray, and seek my face, and turn from their wicked ways: then I will hear from heaven, and will forgive their sin, and will heal their land*—2 Chronicles 7:14, italics added.

What a blessed promise! If we repent and pray, we can change the very destiny of America. *No one is exempt from this great commission!* We must humble ourselves and pray.

GETTING STARTED

When people believe in *themselves,* they will do things their way. When they believe in God, they will *pray!* It takes time to become so "kingdom minded" that we are propelled into an attitude of teamwork with the Lord and fellow believers. That state of mind comes through years of being an intercessor. It is most predominant in mature intercessors.

A multitude of feelings, emotions, attitudes, and attributes need to change in young Christians before they walk daily in the grace to lay down their desires, needs, and even their lives if need be to give one precious treasure for God's Kingdom. The whole of that remarkable transformation is developed from beginning to end with "knowing God."

Most people start a prayer life because of a need—not necessarily because they believe in victory but because they *need* victory. That's all right. Just as need is the mother of invention, need is the mother of prayer.

I began this book with chapters on encouragement to help you look beyond your need, into God's need to be the source and the answer to your prayers. In getting our perspectives into alignment, faith is released and hope is born so that we will win the victor's wreath.

Living in a world dealing with tangibles every day makes learning to deal in a world of intangibles—hope, faith, love, and reverence for a God you have never seen—a difficult transition to make. It's easy to purchase a stereo knowing the benefit of valuable hours of enjoyment you'll receive from having it available in your home. But to spend an hour in prayer with only the *hope* of future benefit is difficult to fathom. Even after many victories, each new need becomes a challenge in itself. The transition, however, is both possible and necessary.

The transition is possible because we know that our intangible Lord is the One who created all these tangible things around us. Most importantly, He created *you*. No one knows you better than God does; nor does anyone love you more. In the beginning of your walk with Jesus, you wanted *your* will more than His because that was a way of life. It takes time to discover how much of your life is controlled by your will rather than His. Since His ways are not our ways, it takes even longer to learn the difference so we can be controlled by the Holy Spirit. Thus, learning to yield to His will, even when you don't understand but simply decide to trust His way, is best.

The transition is necessary because without it you'll never be powerful in prayer or victorious against the powers of the evil one on a consistent basis. It is necessary because God is Spirit. Therefore, obtaining the victor's wreath for running and winning the race will only come through spiritual power and fortitude.

Last, but not least, it is necessary because God is looking for those who will worship Him in spirit. This can only take place in prayer. With every new touch of God on your heart, you will grow in the desire to know Him and experience Him more; and you will want to leave more and more of the world behind. Subsequently, you'll grow in the desire to bring others into these experiences of love and expressions of freedom that only God can give.

By this time, your prayer life will have been elevated from the infancy of need to the desire to give—to transform the world of hurting people into one of beauty. With it will come new growth new knowledge, and new power.

KNOWING GOD'S HEART

The desire to give God to others will push you through hindrances to your prayer life that nothing else can do. The closer you grow to the Lord, the more you will be sensitized to the needs of others. You'll *know* His heart and long to meet those needs. Strongholds that Satan seeks to put up to stop you will cause a holy anger to be aroused in you instead of self-pity. They will make you plow through each and every obstacle with new determination to win your valued victor's wreath.

Finally, knowing God is a priceless treasure. A treasure that can only be discovered through prayer. No price is too great to pay to become truly one with the unsearchable expanses of His loving heart. He alone can put spring in the air of the most horrible day. He alone can teach you how to draw from His matchless grace to overcome every obstacle put in your way. His beauty is beyond compare.

I've sought to share some of the God I know with you to encourage you to desire Him and all He affords more than anything else that is in your world. I desire that you understand the God of liberty to the point that you become enthralled with Him—so enthralled that the tentacles of the world can't hold you any more. There is no prison cell, no hospital bed, no oppressive relationship, no physical handicap—nothing—that can keep you from experiencing the magnificent God of liberty of the Bible. The only thing you need is *desire*.

As you grow in immensity of desire to know Him and to become one with Him. He will reveal Himself and lead you into the knowledge of the wonders of His person. As you continue a life of prayer and obedience, He will eventually lead you into union with Himself and bring you into the walk of the Spirit and the overcoming life. The overcoming life is waiting for each one of us. There is no need to ever let go of that lofty desire. But it can only be realized through prayer. I can't put it more beautifully or powerfully than the apostle Paul when he wrote:

> *Who shall separate us from the love of Christ? Shall tribulation, or distress, or persecution, or famine, or nakedness, or peril or sword?...But in all these things we overwhelmingly conquer through Him who loved us. For I am convinced that neither death, nor life, nor angels, nor principalities, nor things present, nor things to come, nor powers, nor height, nor depth, nor any other created thing, shall be able to separate us from the love of God, which is in Christ Jesus our Lord—*
> Romans 8:35, 37-39

Name _____

Address _____

City/State/Zip _____

Phone (_____)_____ Today's Date _____

All Materials Are FREE of Charge.
Purchaser is Liable for Postage & Handling.

Canadian Customers Please Make Checks Payable To: NITA JOHNSON

NO.	TITLE
S100	Gifts of Fire
S101	Keys of Faith
S102	The Kingdom
S103	Christ and the Bride
S104	The Liverty of Grace
S105	Prayer Power
S106	Melchisedec
S107	Prophetic Insight II
S108	Prophetic Insight III
S109	Prophetic Insight IV
S110	Prophetic Insight V
S111	Intercession
S112	The Wonders of Prayer
S113	Unity
S114	Love Revival
S115	Victory Over the Curste
S116	Problem or Opportunity
S117	Aglow with the Spirt
S118	Revelation Through Meditation
S119	Holiness Unto the Lord
S120	Secrets of Prayer
S121	Prophecy Conference
S122	Prophetic Intercessors Conference
100	Peter
101	For Singles Only
102	Spirit of Giving
BOOK	Prepare for the Winds of Change II
BOOK	The Ever Speaking Voice of God
BOOK	Putting on the Breastplate of Righteousness
BOOK	The Overcoming Life Through Prayer

POSTAGE & HANDLING (call office for costs) $ _____

Future Publications soon to be released:
   • Canticles of the Exchanged Life.   • Winning the Vision.

THE WORLD FOR JESUS MINISTRIES, INC.
MSC #402
497 - N. Clovis Ave. #202
Clovis, CA 93611-0373

If you would like to receive our bi-monthly newsletter entitled: *Prophetic Insight and Family Focus*, free of charge please let us know.

It is a prophetic bulletin geared toward the family and will help you prepare for the days ahead.

New Address as of September 1998.

EAGLE'S NEST PUBLISHING
MSC #402
497 - N. Clovis Ave. #202
Clovis, CA 93611-0373

.